15 MINUTE
FRENCH

15 MINUTE
FRENCH
LEARN IN JUST 12 WEEKS

Caroline Lemoine

Penguin
Random
House

Senior Editor Angeles Gavira
Project Art Editor Vanessa Marr
DTP Designer John Goldsmid
Producer Nancy-Jane Maun
Publishing Manager Liz Wheeler
Managing Art Editor Philip Ormerod
Publishing Director Jonathan Metcalf
Art Director Bryn Walls

**Language content for Dorling Kindersley by
g-and-w publishing**

**Produced for Dorling Kindersley by
Schermuly Design Co.**

First published in Great Britain in 2005 by
Dorling Kindersley Limited
80 Strand, London WC2R 0RL
Penguin Group (UK)

15 13 11 10 12 14
015-HD024-May/2013-book
011-187523-Jan/13-pack

A CIP catalogue record is available for this book
from the British Library.
ISBN 978-1-4093-7760-3

15-Minute French is available as a book on its own,
in an audio pack with two CDs, or as part of a
complete language pack.

Printed and bound in China

A WORLD OF IDEAS:
SEE ALL THERE IS TO KNOW
www.dk.com

CONTENTS

How to use this book

The main part of the book is devoted to 12 themed chapters, broken down into five 15-minute daily lessons, the last of which is a revision lesson. So, in just 12 weeks you will have completed the course. A concluding reference section contains a menu guide and English-to-French and French-to-English dictionaries.

Warm up
Each day starts with a one-minute warm up that encourages you to recall vocabulary or phrases you have learned previously. To the right of the heading bar you will see how long you need to spend on each exercise.

Instructions
Each exercise is numbered and introduced by instructions that explain what to do. In some cases additional information is given about the language point being covered.

Cultural/Conversational tip
These panels provide additional insights into life in France and language usage.

Text styles
Distinctive text styles differentiate French and English, and the pronunciation guide (see right).

How to use the flap
The book's cover flaps allow you to conceal the French so that you can test whether you have remembered correctly.

In conversation
Illustrated dialogues reflecting how vocabulary and phrases are used in everyday situations appear throughout the book.

Review and repeat
A recap of selected elements of previous lessons helps to reinforce your knowledge.

---

18   WEEK 2

1 Warm up (1 minute)

Count to ten (pp.10-11).

Remind yourself how to say "hello" and "goodbye". (pp.8-9)

Ask "Do you have a baguette?" (pp.14-15)

AU CAFÉ
In the café

In a typical French café you can either sit at the counter, which is cheaper, or have waiter service at a table. Tipping is the norm if you're happy with the service, but a few coins will be enough. Food is not usually served, although you can often get bread and croissants in the mornings.

2 Words to remember (5 minutes)

Look at the words below and say them out loud a few times. Cover the French with the flap and try to remember the French for each item. Practise the words on the picture also.

le café crème	coffee with
luh kafay krem	frothy milk
le grand café	large black
luh groh kafay	coffee
le thé	black tea
luh tay	
le thé au lait	tea with milk
luh tay oh lay	

la confiture
lah confeetyur
jam

le café
luh cafeh
small black coffee

le sucre
luh sookruh
sugar

Cultural tip A standard coffee is small and black. You'll need to ask if you want it any other way. If you like milk in your tea, you'll need to specify cold milk (**lait froid/** lay frwah), otherwise you are likely to get a jug of hot milk.

3 In conversation (4 minutes)

Bonjour. Je voudrais un café au lait, s'il vous plaît.
bonjoor. juh voodray uñ kafay oh lay, seel voo play

Hello. I would like a white coffee, please.

C'est tout madame?
say too ma-dam

Is that all madam?

Vous avez des croissants?
voo zavay day krossoñ

Do you have any croissants?

---

36   WEEK 3   MAKING ARRANGEMENTS   37

Réponses Answers (Cover with flap)

1 Sums
2 I want

RÉVISEZ ET RÉPÉTEZ
Review and repeat

1 Sums (4 minutes)
2 I want (3 minutes)
3 Telephones (4 minutes)
4 When? (3 minutes)
5 Time (4 minutes)

Réponses Answers (Cover with flap)

3 Telephones
4 When?
5 Time

Useful phrases
Selected phrases
relevant to the topic
help you speak and
understand.

EATING AND DRINKING 19

4 Useful phrases (5 minutes)

Learn these phrases. Read the English under the
pictures and say the phrase in French as shown on
the right. Then conceal the French with the cover
flap and test yourself.

I'd like a large black
coffee, please.

Je voudrais un grand
café, s'il vous plaît.
juh voodray uñ groñ kafay,
seel voo play

Is that all?

C'est tout?
say too

I'll have a croissant.

Je prends un croissant.
juh pron uñ krossoñ

How much is that?

C'est combien?
say koñbyañ

Two croissants then. How
much is that?

Alors deux croissants.
C'est combien?
alor duh krossoñ, say
koñbyañ

Four euros, please.

Quatre euros, s'il vous
plaît.
katruh uroh, seel voo play

Say it
In these exercises you are
asked to apply what you
have learned using
different vocabulary.

6 Say it (2 minutes)

Do you go near the
train station?

The fruit market, please.

When's the next coach
to Calais?

Pronunciation guide

Many French sounds will already be familiar to you,
but a few require special attention. Take note of
how these letters are pronounced:

r   a French **r** is pronounced in the back of
the throat, producing a sound a little
like gargling

j   a French **j** is soft like the sound in
the middle of *pleasure* (as opposed
to the hard English *j* as in *major*)

n   **n** is pronounced nasally when in the
combination **on**, **an** or **in**. Imagine saying *huh*
through your nose. The nasal **n** is shown in the
pronunciation with this symbol: **ñ**

ch   **ch** in French is equivalent to *sh* in English, as in
ship

er/ez these endings are pronounced *ay* as in *play*

Pay attention also to these vowel sounds as they may
vary from English:

    i   as the English *keep*
    au   as the English *over*
    eu   as the English *fur*
    oi   as the English *wag*

Below each French word or phrase you will find
a pronunciation transcription. Read this, bearing
in mind the tips above, and you will achieve a
comprehensible result. But remember that the
transcription can only ever be an approximation
and that there is no real substitute for listening
to and mimicking native speakers.

Dictionary
A mini-dictionary
provides ready reference
from English to French
and French to English
for 2,500 words.

146 DICTIONARY

DICTIONARY
French to English

The gender of French nouns listed here is indicated by the abbreviations "(m)"
and "(f)", for masculine and feminine. Plural nouns are indicated by "(m pl)" or
"(f pl)". French adjectives (adj) vary according to the gender and number of the
word they describe; the masculine form is shown here. In most cases, you add
an **-e** to the masculine form to make it feminine. Certain endings use a different
rule: masculine adjectives that end in **-x** adopt an **-se** ending in the feminine form,
while those that end in **-ien** change to **-ienne**. Some feminine adjectives that do
not follow these rules are shown here and follow the abbreviation "(fem)". For
the plural form, a (silent) **-s** is usually added.

Menu guide
Use this guide as a reference
for food terminology and
popular French dishes.

128 MENU GUIDE

MENU GUIDE

This guide lists the most common terms you may
encounter on French menus or when shopping for
food. If you can't find an exact phrase, try looking
up its component parts.

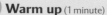

BONJOUR
Hello

1 **Warm up** (1 minute)

The Warm Up panel appears at the beginning of each topic. Use it to reinforce what you have already learned and to prepare yourself for moving ahead with the new subject.

In France it is part of the culture to greet family and friends with kisses on the cheek. The number of kisses varies from two to four. For example, it is usually three kisses in the south but two in Brittany. In more formal situations, a handshake is part of the normal greeting.

Salut!
saloo
Hi!

2 **Words to remember** (2 minutes)

Look at these polite expressions and say them aloud. Cover the text on the left with the cover flap and try to remember the French for each item. Check your answers.

Bonjour. *boñjoor*	Hello.
Bonsoir/bonne nuit. *boñswar/bon nwee*	Good evening/ good night.
Je m'appelle Jean. *juh mapell joñ*	My name is Jean.
Enchanté (men)/ **Enchantée** (women). *oñshontay*	Pleased to meet you.

Cultural tip The French tend to greet people with **monsieur** (*sir*), **madame** (*madam*, for older women), or **mademoiselle** (*miss*, for younger women) much more than most English-speakers would.

3 **In conversation: formal** (3 minutes)

Bonjour. Je m'appelle Céline Legrand.
boñjoor. juh mapell seleen luhgroñ

Hello. My name's Céline Legrand.

Bonjour madame. Monsieur Rossi, enchanté.
boñjoor ma-dam. musyuh rossee, oñshontay

Hello (madam). Mr Rossi, pleased to meet you.

Enchantée.
oñshontay

Pleased to meet you.

4 Put into practice (3 minutes)

Join in this conversation. Read the French beside the pictures on the left and then follow the instructions to make your reply. Then test yourself by concealing the answers on the right with the cover flap.

Bonjour monsieur.
boñjoor musyuh.

Bonjour mademoiselle.
boñjoor mad-mwazel

Hello sir.

Say: Hello mademoiselle.

Je m'appelle Martine.
juh mapell marteen.

Enchanté.
oñshontay

My name is Martine.

Say: Pleased to meet you.

5 Useful phrases (3 minutes)

Familiarize yourself with these phrases. Read them aloud several times and try to memorize them. Conceal the French with the cover flap and test yourself.

Goodbye.	**Au revoir.** *ovwar*
See you soon.	**A bientôt.** *ah byañtoe*
See you tomorrow.	**A demain.** *ah dumañ*
Thank you (very much).	**Merci (beaucoup).** *mairsee (bohkoo)*

6 In conversation: informal (3 minutes)

Alors, à demain?
alor, ah dumañ

So, see you tomorrow?

Oui, au revoir.
wee, ovwar

Yes, goodbye.

Au revoir. A bientôt.
ovwar. ah byañtoe

Goodbye. See you soon.

LES RELATIONS
Relatives

1 **Warm up** (1 minute)

Say "hello" and "goodbye" in French. (pp.8–9)

Now say "My name is..." (pp.8–9)

Say "sir" and "madam". (pp.8–9)

In French the same word is used for relationships by marriage: **beau-père** means both father-in-law and step-father, and **belle-fille** means daughter-in-law and stepdaughter. The French for *the* is **le** or **la**, and *a* is **un** or **une**, depending on whether the word is masculine or feminine (see below).

2 **Match and repeat** (5 minutes)

Look at the people in this scene and match their numbers with the vocabulary list at the side. Read the French words aloud. Now, cover the list with the flap and test yourself.

❶ **le grand-père**
   luh groñpair

❷ **le frère**
   luh frair

❸ **la sœur**
   lah sur

❹ **le père**
   luh pair

❺ **la mère**
   lah mair

❻ **la grand-mère**
   lah groñmair

❼ **le fils**
   luh fees

❽ **la fille**
   lah feeyuh

❶ grandfather

brother ❷

❸ sister

❹ father

❺ mother

grandmother ❻   ❼ son   ❽ daughter

Conversational tip In French, things as well as people are masculine (m) or feminine (f). For example, *wine* is masculine (**le vin**) but *car* is feminine (**la voiture**). For the plural **les** is used for both masculine and feminine. In this book (m) or (f) indicates the gender after a plural.

3 Words to remember: relatives (4 minutes)

le mari
luh maree
husband

la femme
lah fam
wife

Look at these words and say them aloud. Conceal the text on the right with the cover flap and try to remember the French. Check your answers. Then practise the phrases below.

Nous sommes mariés.
Noo som mareeay
We are married.

sister-in-law/ stepsister	**la belle-sœur** *lah bell sur*
brother-in-law/ stepbrother	**le beau-frère** *luh boe frair*
half-sister	**la demi-sœur** *lah dumee sur*
half-brother	**le demi-frère** *luh dumee frair*
children	**les enfants** (m) *lay zoñfoñ*
I have four children.	**J'ai quatre enfants.** *jay katruh oñfoñ*
I have two stepdaughters.	**J'ai deux belles-filles.** *jay duh bell feeyuh*

4 Words to remember: numbers (3 minutes)

Memorize these words. Now cover the French and test yourself.

Be careful with the pronunciation of **deux** and **trois**. When you say them in front of a word that starts with a vowel, you need to say an extra "z" sound – for example, **deux enfants** (two children) is pronounced *duh zoñfoñ*, and **trois éclairs** (three eclairs), *trwah zayclair*. This is also true of other words.

one	**un/une** *uñ* (m)/*oon* (f)
two	**deux** *duh*
three	**trois** *trwah*
four	**quatre** *katruh*
five	**cinq** *sank*
six	**six** *sees*
seven	**sept** *set*
eight	**huit** *weet*
nine	**neuf** *nurf*
ten	**dix** *dees*

5 Say it (2 minutes)

I have five sons.

I have three sisters and a brother.

I have two stepsons.

1 Warm up (1 minute)

Say the French for as many members of the family as you can. (pp.10-11)

Say "I have two sons". (pp.10-11)

MA FAMILLE
My family

The French have two ways of saying *you*: **vous** for people you meet or don't know very well and **tu** for family and friends. Similarly, there are different words for *your*. The words for *my* and *your* also change depending on whether they relate to masculine, feminine, or plural nouns.

2 Words to remember (5 minutes)

Say these words out loud a few times. Cover the French with the flap and try to remember the French word for each item.

mon *moñ*	my (with masculine)
ma *mah*	my (with feminine)
mes *may*	my (with plural)
ton *toñ*	your (informal, with masculine)
ta *tah*	your (informal, with feminine)
tes *tay*	your (informal, with plural)
votre *votruh*	your (formal, with masculine or feminine)
vos *voe*	your (formal, with plural)

Voici mes parents.
vwasee may paroñ
These are my parents.

3 In conversation (4 minutes)

Vous avez des enfants?
voo zavay day zoñfoñ

Do you have any children?

Oui, j'ai deux filles.
wee, jay duh feeyuh

Yes, I have two daughters.

**Voici mes filles.
Et vous?**
*vwasee may feeyuh.
ay voo*

These are my daughters.
And you?

Conversational tip The French usually ask a question by simply raising the pitch of the voice at the end of a statement - for example, **Vous voulez un café?** (*Do you want a coffee?*). You could also ask the same question by inverting the verb and subject: **Voulez-vous un café?**. Or you can put **Est-ce que** in front of the sentence **Est-ce que vous voulez un café?**

4 Useful phrases (3 minutes)

Read these phrases aloud several times and try to memorize them. Conceal the French with the cover flap and test yourself.

Do you have any brothers? (formal)	**Vous avez des frères?** *voo zavay day frair*
Do you have any brothers? (informal)	**Tu as des frères?** *tew ah day frair*
This is my husband.	**Voici mon mari.** *vwasee moñ maree*
That's my wife.	**C'est ma femme.** *say mah fam*
Is that your sister? (formal)	**C'est votre sœur?** *say votruh sur*
Is that your sister? (informal)	**C'est ta sœur?** *say tah sur*

5 Say it (2 minutes)

J'ai un beau-fils.
jay uñ boe fees

I have a stepson.

Do you have any brothers and sisters? (formal)

Do you have any children? (informal)

I have two sisters.

This is my wife.

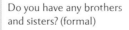

1 Warm up (1 minute)

Say "See you soon".
(pp.8-9)

Say "I am married"
(pp.10-11) and
"I have a daughter".
(pp.12-13)

ETRE ET AVOIR
To be and to have

There are some essential verbs for you to learn in this course. You can use these to construct a large variety of useful phrases. The first two are **être** (*to be*) and **avoir** (*to have*). Learn them carefully as French verbs change more than English ones according to the pronoun (I, you, etc.) used.

2 Etre: to be (5 minutes)

Familiarize yourself with the different forms of être (*to be*). Use the cover flaps to test yourself and, when you are confident, practise the sample sentences below.

je suis *juh swee*	I am
tu es *tew ay*	you are (informal singular)
il/elle est *eel/el ay*	he/she is
nous sommes *noo som*	we are
vous êtes *voo zet*	you are (formal singular or plural)
ils/elles sont *eel/el soñ*	they are

Je suis anglaise.
juh swee zonglayz
I'm English.

Je suis fatigué(e). *juh swee fatigay*	I'm tired.
Elle est heureuse? *el ay tururz*	Is she happy?
Nous sommes français. *noo som froñsay*	We're French.

3 Avoir: to have (5 minutes)

Practise **avoir** (*to have*) and the sample sentences, then test yourself.

I have	**j'ai**
	jay
you have (informal singular)	**tu as**
	tew ah
he/she has	**il/elle a**
	eel/el ah
we have	**nous avons**
	noo zavoñ
you have (formal singular or plural)	**vous avez**
	voo zavay
they have	**ils/elles ont**
	eel/el zoñ

Il a deux baguettes.
eel ah duh baget
He has two baguettes.

He has a meeting.	**Il a un rendez-vous.**
	eel ah uñ roñday-voo
Do you have a mobile phone?	**Vous avez un portable?**
	voo zavay uñ portabluh
How many brothers and sisters do you have?	**Vous avez combien de frères et sœurs?**
	voo zavay koñbyañ duh frair ay sur

4 Negatives (4 minutes)

To make a sentence negative in French, put **ne** in front of the verb and **pas** just after: **nous ne sommes pas anglais** (*we are not English*). If **ne** is followed by a vowel, it becomes **n'**: **je n'ai pas d'enfants** (*I don't have any children*). But many French people drop the **ne** when they're talking, so you'll just hear **nous sommes pas** (*we aren't*), **j'ai pas** (*I haven't*), and so on. Read these sentences aloud, then cover the French with the flap and test yourself.

le vélo
luh vayloe
bicycle

He's not married.	**Il n'est pas marié.**
	eel nay pah mariyay
I am not sure.	**Je ne suis pas sûr(e).**
	juh nuh swee pah syur
We don't have any children.	**Nous n'avons pas d'enfants.**
	noo navoñ pah doñfoñ

Je n'ai pas de voiture.
juh nay pas duh vwatyur
I don't have a car.

RÉVISEZ ET RÉPÉTEZ
Review and repeat

1 How many?

❶ trois
trwah

❷ neuf
nurf

❸ quatre
katruh

❹ deux
duh

❺ huit
weet

❻ dix
dees

❼ cinq
sank

❽ sept
set

❾ six
sees

1 How many? (2 minutes)

Cover the answers with the flap. Then say these French numbers out loud. Check you have remembered the French correctly.

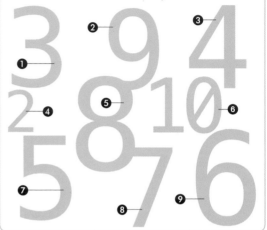

2 Hello

❶ Bonjour. Je
m'appelle... [your
name].
boñjoor. juh mapell...

❷ Enchanté(e).
oñshontay

❸ Oui, et j'ai deux fils.
Et vous?
*wee, ay jay duh fees.
ay voo*

❹ Au revoir.
A demain.
ovwar. ah dumañ

2 Hello (4 minutes)

You meet someone in a formal situation. Join in the conversation, replying in French according to the English prompts.

Bonjour. Je m'appelle Nicole.
❶ Answer the greeting and give your name.

Voici mon mari, Henri.
❷ Say "Pleased to meet you".

Vous êtes marié(e)?
❸ Say "Yes, and I have two sons. And you?"

Nous avons trois filles.
❹ Say "Goodbye. See you tomorrow".

3 To have or be (5 minutes)

Fill in the blanks with the correct form of **avoir** (*to have*) or **être** (*to be*). Check you have remembered the French correctly.

❶ Je _____ anglaise.

❷ Nous _____ quatre enfants.

❸ Elle _____ une belle-fille.

❹ Vous _____ rendez-vous?

❺ Il n' _____ pas fatigué.

❻ Je n' _____ pas de portable.

❼ Tu n' _____ pas sûr?

❽ Nous _____ français.

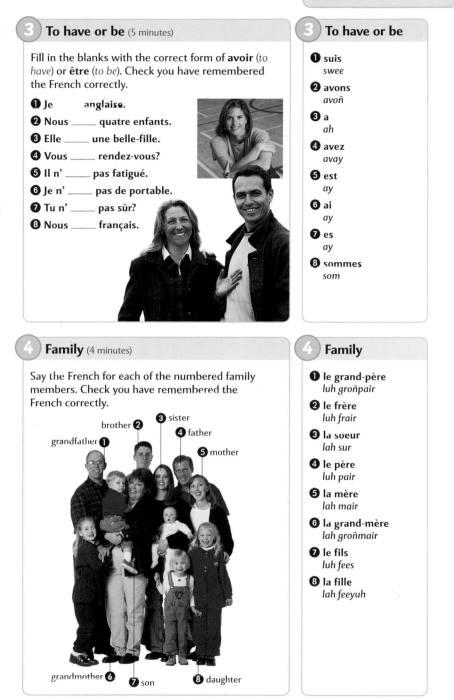

3 To have or be

❶ **suis**
swee

❷ **avons**
avoñ

❸ **a**
ah

❹ **avez**
avay

❺ **est**
ay

❻ **ai**
ay

❼ **es**
ay

❽ **sommes**
som

4 Family (4 minutes)

Say the French for each of the numbered family members. Check you have remembered the French correctly.

brother ❷ ❸ sister
grandfather ❶ ❹ father
❺ mother

grandmother ❻ ❼ son ❽ daughter

4 Family

❶ **le grand-père**
luh groñpair

❷ **le frère**
luh frair

❸ **la sœur**
lah sur

❹ **le père**
luh pair

❺ **la mère**
lah mair

❻ **la grand-mère**
lah groñmair

❼ **le fils**
luh fees

❽ **la fille**
lah feeyuh

AU CAFÉ
In the café

1 **Warm up** (1 minute)

Count to ten (pp.10-11).

Remind yourself how to say "hello" and "goodbye". (pp.8-9)

Ask "Do you have a baguette?" (pp.14-15)

In a typical French café you can either sit at the counter, which is cheaper, or have waiter service at a table. Tipping is the norm if you're happy with the service, but a few coins will be enough. Food is not usually served, although you can often get bread and croissants in the mornings.

2 **Words to remember** (5 minutes)

Look at the words below and say them out loud a few times. Cover the French with the flap and try to remember the French for each item. Practise the words on the picture also.

le café crème *luh kafay krem*	coffee with frothy milk
le grand café *luh groñ kafay*	large black coffee
le thé *luh tay*	black tea
le thé au lait *luh tay oh lay*	tea with milk

la confiture
lah coñfeetyur
jam

le café
luh cafeh
small black coffee

le sucre
luh sookruh
sugar

Cultural tip A standard coffee is small and black. You'll need to ask if you want it any other way. If you like milk in your tea, you'll need to specify cold milk (**lait froid/** lay frwah), otherwise you are likely to get a jug of hot milk.

3 **In conversation** (4 minutes)

Bonjour. Je voudrais un café au lait, s'il vous plaît.
bonjoor. juh voodray uñ kafay oh lay, seel voo play

Hello. I would like a white coffee, please.

C'est tout madame?
say too ma-dam

Is that all madam?

Vous avez des croissants?
voo zavay day krossoñ

Do you have any croissants?

4 Useful phrases (5 minutes)

Learn these phrases. Read the English under the pictures and say the phrase in French as shown on the right. Then conceal the French with the cover flap and test yourself.

le pain
luh pañ
bread

Je voudrais un grand café, s'il vous plaît.
juh voodray uñ groñ kafay, seel voo play

I'd like a large black coffee, please.

C'est tout?
say too

Is that all?

Je prends un croissant.
juh pron uñ krossoñ

I'll have a croissant.

le café au lait
luh kafay oh lay
large coffee with milk

C'est combien?
say koñbyañ

How much is that?

Oui, bien sûr.
wee, byañ syur

Yes, certainly.

Alors deux croissants. C'est combien?
alor duh krossoñ. say koñbyañ

Two croissants then. How much is that?

Quatre euros, s'il vous plaît.
katruh uroh, seel voo play

Four euros, please.

1 Warm up (1 minute)

Say "I'd like".
(pp.18-19)

Say "I don't have a brother". (pp.14-15)

Ask "Do you have any croissants?" (pp.18-19)

AU RESTAURANT
In the restaurant

There is a variety of different types of eating place in France. In a **café** you can find a few snacks. A **brasserie** is a traditional restaurant; the service is fast and there's usually no need to book. In the more formal gastronomic restaurants, it is necessary to book and to dress smartly.

2 Words to remember (3 minutes)

Memorize these words. Conceal the French with the cover flap and test yourself.

la carte *lah kart*	menu
la carte des vins *lah kart day vañ*	wine list
les entrées (f) *lay zontray*	starters
les plats (m) *lay plah*	main courses
les desserts (m) *lay dessair*	desserts
le déjeuner *luh dayjunay*	lunch
le dîner *luh deenay*	dinner
le petit-déjeuner *luh puhtee dayjunay*	breakfast

cup **7**

saucer **8**

5 spoon

6 knife

fork **4**

3 In conversation (4 minutes)

Bonjour. Je voudrais une table pour quatre.
boñjoor. juh voodray oon tabluh poor katruh

Hello. I would like a table for four.

Vous avez une réservation?
voo zavay oon raysairvasyoñ

Do you have a reservation?

Oui, au nom de Smith.
wee, oh noñ duh Smith

Yes, in the name of Smith.

4 **Match and repeat** (5 minutes)

Look at the numbered items in this table setting and match them with the French words on the right. Read the French words aloud. Now, conceal the French with the cover flap and test yourself.

glass ❶

❷ napkin

plate ❸

❶ **le verre**
luh vair

❷ **la serviette**
lah sairvyet

❸ **l'assiette** (f)
lasyet

❹ **la fourchette**
lah forshet

❺ **la cuillère**
lah kweeyair

❻ **le couteau**
luh kootoe

❼ **la tasse**
lah tass

❽ **la soucoupe**
lah sookoop

5 **Useful phrases** (2 minutes)

Learn these phrases and then test yourself using the cover flap to conceal the French.

What do you have for dessert?	**Qu'est ce que vous avez comme dessert?** *keskuh voo zavay kom dessair*
The bill, please.	**L'addition, s'il vous plaît.** *ladeesyoñ, seel voo play*

D'accord. Quelle table vous préférez?
dakor. kel tabluh voo prayfayray

Fine. Which table would you like?

Près de la fenêtre, s'il vous plaît.
pray duh lah fenetruh, seel voo play

Near the window, please.

Mais bien sûr. Suivez-moi.
may byañ syur. sweevay mwah

But of course. Follow me.

VOULOIR
To want

1 Warm up (1 minute)

What are "breakfast", "lunch", and "dinner" in French? (pp.20-1)

Say "I", "you" (informal), "he", "she", "we", "you" (plural/formal), "they" (masculine), "they" (feminine). (pp.14-15)

In this section, you will learn the present tense of a verb that is essential to everyday conversation - **vouloir** (*to want*) - as well as a useful polite form, **je voudrais** (*I would like*). Remember to use this form when requesting something because **je veux** (*I want*) may sound too strong.

2 Vouloir: to want (6 minutes)

Say the different forms of **vouloir** (*to want*) aloud. Use the cover flaps to test yourself and, when you are confident, practise the sample sentences below.

je veux *juh vuh*	I want
tu veux *tew vuh*	you want (informal)
il/elle veut *eel/el vuh*	he/she wants
nous voulons *noo vooloñ*	we want
vous voulez *voo voolay*	you want (formal/plural)
ils/elles veulent *eel/el verl*	they want
Tu veux du vin? *tew vuh dew vañ*	Do you want some wine?
Elle veut une nouvelle voiture. *el vuh oon noovel vwatyur*	She wants a new car.
Nous voulons aller en vacances. *noo vooloñ zallay oñ vakons*	We want to go on holiday.

Je veux des bonbons.
juh vuh day boñ-boñ
I want some sweets.

Conversational tip To say *some*, **de** (*of*) combines with **le**, **la**, or **les** to produce **du** for the masculine, **de la** for feminine, or **des** for the plural, as in **du café**, **de la confiture**, and **des citrons** (*lemons*). If the sentence is negative, use only **de**, as in **Il n'y a pas de café**. In the same way, **à** (*to*) combines with **le**, **la**, or **les** to produce **au** for the masculine, **à la** for the feminine, and **aux** for the plural.

3 Polite requests (4 minutes)

There is a form of **je veux** (*I want*) used for polite requests: **je voudrais**. Practise the sentences below and then test yourself.

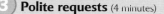

I'd like a beer, please. | **Je voudrais une bière, s'il vous plaît.**
juh voodray oon biyair, seel voo play

I'd like a table for tonight. | **Je voudrais une table pour ce soir.**
juh voodray oon tabluh poor suh swar

I'd like the menu. | **Je voudrais la carte.**
juh voodray lah kart

4 Put into practice (4 minutes)

Join in this conversation. Read the French beside the pictures on the left and then follow the English prompts to make your reply in French. Test yourself by concealing the answers with the cover flap.

Bonsoir, madame. Vous avez une réservation?
boñswar, ma-dam. Voo zavay oon raysairvasyoñ

Good evening, madam. Do you have a reservation?

Say: No, but I would like a table for three, please.

Non, mais je voudrais une table pour trois, s'il vous plaît.
noñ, may juh voodray oon tabluh poor trwah, seel voo play

Fumeur ou non-fumeur?
foomur oo noñ-foomur

Smoking or non-smoking?

Say: I'd like non-smoking, please.

Je voudrais non-fumeur, s'il vous plaît.
juh voodray noñ-foomur, seel voo play

LES PLATS
Dishes

1 **Warm up** (1 minute)

Say "I'm tired" and
"I'm not sure". (pp.14-15)

Ask "Do you have
croissants?" (pp.18-19)

Say "I'd like a white
coffee". (pp.18-19)

France is famous for its cuisine and the quality of
its best restaurants. It also offers a wide variety
of regional dishes. Plenty of garlic and butter are a
feature of many typical dishes. Although traditionally
French cuisine is meat-based, many restaurants now
offer a vegetarian menu.

Cultural tip You will usually have the choice of
eating a set **menu** or ordering **à la carte**. With a set
menu, salad is often a starter and you usually have
to choose between dessert or cheese.

2 **Match and repeat** (4 minutes)

Look at the numbered items and match them to the
French words in the panel on the left. Test yourself
using the cover flap.

1 **les légumes** (m)
lay laygoom

2 **le fruit**
luh froo-wee

3 **le fromage**
luh fromarj

4 **les noix** (f)
lay nwah

5 **la soupe**
lah soop

6 **la volaille**
lah vol-eye

7 **le poisson**
luh pwassoñ

8 **les pâtes** (f)
lay pat

9 **les fruits de mer** (m)
*lay froo-wee
duh mair*

10 **la viande**
lah vee-ond

fruit **2**

vegetables **1**

cheese **3**

5 soup

poultry **6**

8 pasta

9 seafood

3 Words to remember: cooking methods (3 minutes)

Familiarize yourself with these words and then test yourself.

fried	**frit(e)**	*free(t)*
grilled	**grillé(e)**	*greeyay*
roasted	**rôti(e)**	*rotee*
boiled	**bouilli(e)**	*booyee*
steamed	**à la vapeur**	*ah lah vapur*
rare	**saignant(e)**	*say-nyoñ(t)*

Je voudrais mon steak bien cuit.
juh voodray moñ stayk byañ kwee
I'd like my steak well done.

6 Say it (2 minutes)

What is **cassoulet**?

I'm allergic to seafood.

I'd like a beer.

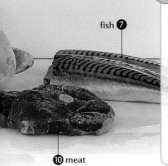

nuts ❹

fish ❼

❿ meat

4 Words to remember: drinks (3 minutes)

Familiarize yourself with these words.

water	**l'eau** (f)	*loe*
fizzy water	**l'eau gazeuse** (f)	*loe gazuz*
still water	**l'eau plate** (f)	*loe plat*
wine	**le vin**	*luh vañ*
beer	**la bière**	*lah biyair*
fruit juice	**le jus de fruits**	*luh joo duh froo-wee*

5 Useful phrases (2 minutes)

Learn these phrases and then test yourself.

I'm a vegetarian	**Je suis végétarien.**	*juh swee vejitah-ryañ*
I'm allergic to nuts.	**Je suis allergique aux noix.**	*juh swee zalurzheek oh nwah*
What are "escargots"?	**Qu'est que c'est les "escargots"?**	*keskuh say lay zeskargoh*

Réponses
Answers (Cover with flap)

RÉVISEZ ET RÉPÉTEZ
Review and repeat

1 At table

❶ les noix
lay nwah

❷ les fruits de mer
lay froo-wee duh mair

❸ la viande
lah vee-ond

❹ le sucre
luh sookruh

❺ le verre
luh vair

1 At table (4 minutes)

Name the numbered items.

❶ nuts
sugar ❹
seafood ❷
meat ❸
glass ❺

2 This is my...

❶ C'est mon mari.
say moñ maree

❷ Voici ma fille.
vwasee mah feeyuh

❸ Ma table est non-fumeur.
mah tabluh ay noñ-foomur

❹ Mes enfants sont fatigués.
may zoñfoñ soñ fatigay

2 This is my... (4 minutes)

Say these phrases in French.
Use **mon**, **ma**, or **mes**.

❶ This is my husband.

❷ Here is my daughter.

❸ My table is non-smoking.

❹ My children are tired.

3 I'd like...

❶ Je voudrais un café.
juh voodray uñ kafay

❷ Je voudrais de la confiture.
juh voodray duh lah coñfeetyur

❸ Je voudrais du pain.
juh voodray doo pañ

❹ Je voudrais un café au lait.
juh voodray uñ kafay oh lay

3 I'd like... (3 minutes)

Say you'd like the following:

bread ❸
jam ❷
❶ black coffee
large coffee ❹ with milk

Réponses
Answers (Cover with flap)

1 At table

6 les pâtes
lay pat

7 le couteau
luh kootoe

8 le fromage
luh fromarj

9 la serviette
lah sairvyet

10 la bière
lah biyair

pasta 6

knife 7

cheese 8

beer 10

napkin 9

4 Restaurant (4 minutes)

You arrive at a restaurant. Join in the conversation, replying in French according to the English prompts.

Bonjour madame, monsieur.
1 Ask for a table for six.

Fumeur ou non-fumeur?
2 Say: non-smoking.

Suivez-moi, s'il vous plaît.
3 Ask for the menu.

Et vous voulez la carte des vins?
4 Say: No. Fizzy water, please.

Voilà.
5 Say: I don't have a glass.

4 Restaurant

1 Bonjour. Je voudrais une table pour six.
boñjoor. juh voodray oon tabluh por sees

2 Non-fumeur.
noñ-foomur

3 La carte, s'il vous plaît.
lah kart, seel voo play

4 Non. De l'eau gazeuse, s'il vous plaît.
noñ. duh loe gazuz, seel voo play

5 Je n'ai pas de verre.
juh nay pah duh vair

LES JOURS ET LES MOIS
Days and months

1 Warm up (1 minute)

Say "he is" and "they are". (pp.14-15)

Say "he is not" and "they are not". (pp.14-15)

What is French for "the children"? (pp.10-11)

In French the *days of the week* (**les jours de semaine**) and *months* (**les mois**) do not have capital letters. The months have similar names to the English. You use **en** with months: **en avril** (*in April*), but not with days.

2 Words to remember: days (5 minutes)

Familiarize yourself with these words and test yourself using the flap.

lundi *luñdee*	Monday
mardi *mardee*	Tuesday
mercredi *mairkrudee*	Wednesday
jeudi *jurdee*	Thursday
vendredi *voñdrudee*	Friday
samedi *samdee*	Saturday
dimanche *deemonsh*	Sunday
aujourd'hui *oh-joordwee*	today
demain *dumañ*	tomorrow
hier *eeyair*	yesterday

Demain, c'est lundi.
dumañ, say luñdee
Tomorrow is Monday.

3 Useful phrases: days (2 minutes)

Learn these phrases and then test yourself using the cover flap.

La réunion n'est pas mardi. *lah rayoonyoñ nay pah mardee*	The meeting isn't on Tuesday.
Je travaille le dimanche. *juh trav-eye luh deemonsh*	I work on Sundays.

4 Words to remember: months (5 minutes)

Familiarize yourself with these words and test yourself using the flap.

Notre anniversaire de mariage est en juillet.
notruh aneevairsair duh mareeaj ay toñ jweeyay
Our wedding anniversary is in July.

Noël est en décembre.
nowel ay toñ daysombruh
Christmas is in December.

January	**janvier**	*joñvyay*
February	**février**	*fevreeyay*
March	**mars**	*mars*
April	**avril**	*avreel*
May	**mai**	*may*
June	**juin**	*jwañ*
July	**juillet**	*jweeyay*
August	**août**	*oot*
September	**septembre**	*septombruh*
October	**octobre**	*oktobruh*
November	**novembre**	*novombruh*
December	**décembre**	*daysombruh*
month	**le mois**	*luh mwah*
year	**l'an** (m)	*loñ*

5 Useful phrases: months (2 minutes)

Learn these phrases and then test yourself using the cover flap.

My children are on holiday in August. **Mes enfants sont en vacances en août.**
may zoñfoñ soñ toñ vakons oñ oot

My birthday is in June. **Mon anniversaire est en juin.**
moñ naneevairsair ay toñ jwañ

L'HEURE ET LES NOMBRES
Time and numbers

1 Warm up (1 minute)

Count in French from 1 to 10. (pp.10-11)

Say "I have a reservation". (pp.20-1)

Say "The meeting is on Wednesday". (pp.28-9)

The 12-hour clock is used in everyday speech while the 24-hour clock is employed in stations and airports, etc. While in English the minutes are first (*ten to five*), in French the hour is first: **dix heures moins cinq** (*ten minus five*).

2 Words to remember: time (4 minutes)

Memorize how to tell the time in French.

une heure *oon ur*	one o'clock
une heure cinq *oon ur sank*	five past one
une heure et quart *oon ur ay kar*	quarter past one
une heure vingt *oon ur vañ*	twenty past one
une heure et demie *oon ur ay dumee*	half past one
deux heures moins le quart *duh zur mwañ luh kar*	quarter to two
deux heures moins dix *duh zur mwañ dees*	ten to two

3 Useful phrases (2 minutes)

Learn these phrases and then test yourself using the cover flap.

Quelle heure est-il? *kel ur ay teel*	What time is it?

A quelle heure voulez-vous le petit déjeuner? *ah kel ur voolay voo luh puhtee dayjunay*	What time do you want breakfast?

J'ai une réservation pour douze heures. *jay oon raysairvasyoñ poor dooz ur*	I have a reservation for twelve o'clock.

4 Words to remember: higher numbers (6 minutes)

In French when you say 21, 31, etc. you say: **vingt-et-un**, **trente-et-un**, and so on. After that just put the numbers together without **et**: **vingt-deux** (22), **quarante-cinq** (45).

70 is **soixante-dix** (*sixty-ten*), 75 is **soixante-quinze** (*sixty-fifteen*), and so on. **Quatre-vingt** (80) means *four-twenties*, and 90 is **quatre-vingt-dix** (*four-twenties-ten*). So 82 is **quatre-vingt-deux** and 97 is **quatre-vingt-dix-sept**.

Ça fait quatre-vingt-cinq euros.
sah fay katruh-vañ-sank uroh
That's eighty-five euros.

eleven	**onze**	*onz*
twelve	**douze**	*dooz*
thirteen	**treize**	*trez*
fourteen	**quatorze**	*katorz*
fifteen	**quinze**	*kanz*
sixteen	**seize**	*sez*
seventeen	**dix-sept**	*deeset*
eighteen	**dix-huit**	*deezweet*
nineteen	**dix-neuf**	*deeznurf*
twenty	**vingt**	*vañ*
thirty	**trente**	*tront*
forty	**quarante**	*karont*
fifty	**cinquante**	*sankont*
sixty	**soixante**	*swasont*
seventy	**soixante-dix**	*swasont-dees*
eighty	**quatre-vingt**	*katruh-vañ*
ninety	**quatre-vingt-dix**	*katruh-vañ-dees*
hundred	**cent**	*soñ*
three hundred	**trois cents**	*trwah soñ*
thousand	**mil**	*meel*
ten thousand	**dix mille**	*dee meel*
two hundred thousand	**deux cent mille**	*duh soñ meel*
one million	**un million**	*oon meel-yoñ*

5 Say it (2 minutes)

twenty-five

sixty-eight

eighty-four

ninety-one

five to ten.

half past eleven.

What time is lunch?

LES RENDEZ-VOUS
Appointments

1 **Warm up** (1 minute)

Say the days of the week.
(pp.28-9)

Say "It's three o'clock".
(pp.30-1)

What's the French for
"today", "tomorrow", and
"yesterday"? (pp.28-9)

Business in France is generally conducted more
formally than in Britain or the United States; always
address business contacts as **vous**. The French tend
to leave the office for the lunch hour, often having a sit-
down meal in a restaurant or, less commonly, at home.

Bienvenue.
byañvenoo
Welcome.

2 **Useful phrases** (5 minutes)

Learn these phrases and then test yourself.

Prenons rendez-vous pour demain. *prunoñ ronday-voo poor dumañ*	Let's meet tomorrow.
Avec qui? *avek kee*	With whom?
Quand êtes-vous libre? *koñ et-voo leebruh*	When are you free?
Je suis désolé(e), je suis occupé(e). *juh swee dayzolay, juh swee zokupay*	I'm sorry, I'm busy.
Pourquoi pas jeudi? *poorkwah pah jurdee*	How about Thursday?
C'est bon pour moi. *say boh poor mwah*	That's good for me.

**la poignée
de main**
*lah pwanyay
duh mañ*
handshake

3 **In conversation** (4 minutes)

Bonjour. J'ai rendez-vous.
boñjoor. jay ronday-voo

Hello. I have an
appointment.

Avec qui?
avek kee

With whom?

Avec Monsieur Le Blanc.
avek musyuh luh bloñ

With Mr Le Blanc.

4 Put into practice (5 minutes)

Join in this conversation. Read the French beside the pictures on the left and then follow the instructions to make your reply. Then test yourself by concealing the answers on the right with the cover flap.

Prenons rendez-vous pour jeudi.
prunoñ ronday-voo poor jurdee

Let's meet on Thursday.

Say: Sorry, I'm busy.

Je suis désolé, je suis occupé.
juh swee dayzolay, juh swee zokupay

Quand êtes-vous libre?
koñ et-voo leebruh

When are you free?

Say: Tuesday afternoon.

Mardi après-midi.
mardee apray meedee

C'est bon pour moi.
say boñ poor mwa

That's good for me.

Ask: What time?

A quelle heure?
ah kel ur

A quatre heures, si c'est bon pour vous.
ah katruh ur see say boñ poor voo

At four o'clock, if that's good for you.

Say: It's good for me.

C'est bon pour moi.
say boñ poor mwah

Très bien. A quelle heure?
tray byañ. ah kel ur

Very good. What time?

A trois heures, mais je suis un peu en retard.
ah trwah zur, may juh swee uñ puh oñ retar

At three o'clock, but I'm a little late.

Ne vous inquiétez pas. Asseyez-vous, je vous en prie.
nuh voo zañkyetay pah. assayay voo, juh voo zon pree

Don't worry. Sit down, please.

AU TÉLÉPHONE
On the telephone

1 Warm up (1 minute)

Say "I'm sorry". (pp.32–3)

What is the French for "I'd like an appointment"? (pp.32–3)

How do you say "with whom?" in French? (pp.32–3)

The emergency number for police, ambulance, or fire services is 112. Telephone cards (**télécartes**) can be used for public phones or private phones by tapping in a code. They are available from post offices and newsagents.

2 Match and repeat (4 minutes)

Match the numbered items to the French in the panel on the left and test yourself.

❶ le chargeur
luh sharjur

❷ les renseignements (m)
lay ronsenyumoñ

❸ le répondeur
luh raypoñdur

❹ le téléphone
luh telayfon

❺ le portable
luh portabluh

❻ la télécarte
lah telaykart

❼ les écouteurs (m)
lay zaykootur

charger ❶

❹ telephone

headphones ❼

mobile ❺

phonecard ❻

3 In conversation (4 minutes)

Allô. Pauline Du Bois à l'appareil.
aloh. pawleen doo bwah ah lap-paray

Hello. Pauline du Bois speaking.

Bonjour. Je voudrais parler à Rachid Djamal.
boñjoor. juh voodray parlay ah rasheed jahmal

Hello. I'd like to speak to Rachid Djamal.

C'est de la part de qui?
say duh lah par duh kee

Who's speaking?

4 Useful phrases (4 minutes)

Practise these phrases. Then test yourself using the cover flap.

Je voudrais une ligne extérieure.
juh voodray oon leenyuh exteree-yur

I'd like an outside line.

directory ❷

Je voudrais parler à Françoise Martin.
juh voodray parlay ah franswahz martañ

I'd like to speak to Françoise Martin.

❸ answering machine

Je peux laisser un message?
juh puh laysay uñ mesarj

Can I leave a message?

5 Say it (2 minutes)

I'd like to speak to Mr Hachart.

Can I leave a message for Emma?

Désolé(e), je me suis trompé(e) de numéro.
dayzolay, juh muh swee trompay duh noomairoe

Sorry I have the wrong number.

Jean Leblanc de l'imprimerie Laporte.
joñ luhbloñ duh lahpreemuree laport

Jean Leblanc of Laporte Printers.

Désolée. La ligne est occupée.
dayzolay. lah leenyuh et okupay

I'm sorry. The line is busy.

Il peut me rappeller, s'il vous plaît?
eel puh muh raplay, seel voo play

Can he call me back, please?

RÉVISEZ ET RÉPÉTEZ
Review and repeat

Réponses
Answers (Cover with flap)

1 Sums

❶ **seize**
sez

❷ **trente-neuf**
tront-nurf

❸ **cinquante-trois**
sankont-trwah

❹ **soixante-quatorze**
swasont-katorz

❺ **quatre-vingt dix-neuf**
katruh-vañ deeznuf

❻ **quarante-et-un**
karont-ay-uñ

1 Sums (4 minutes)

Say the answers
to these sums out
loud in French.
Then check you have
remembered correctly.

❶ $10 + 6 = ?$
❷ $14 + 25 = ?$
❸ $66 - 13 = ?$
❹ $40 + 34 = ?$
❺ $90 + 9 = ?$
❻ $46 - 5 = ?$

3 Telephones (3 minutes)

What are the numbered
items in French?

❶ mobile

phonecard ❸

2 I want...

❶ **voulez**
voolay

❷ **veut**
vuh

❸ **voulons**
vooloñ

❹ **veux**
vuh

❺ **veux**
vuh

❻ **veut**
vuh

2 I want... (3 minutes)

Fill the blanks
with the correct
form of **vouloir**.

❶ Vous _____ un café?

❷ Elle _____ aller en
vacances.

❸ Nous _____ une
table pour trois.

❹ Tu _____ une bière?

❺ Je _____ une nouvelle
voiture.

❻ Il _____ des bonbons.

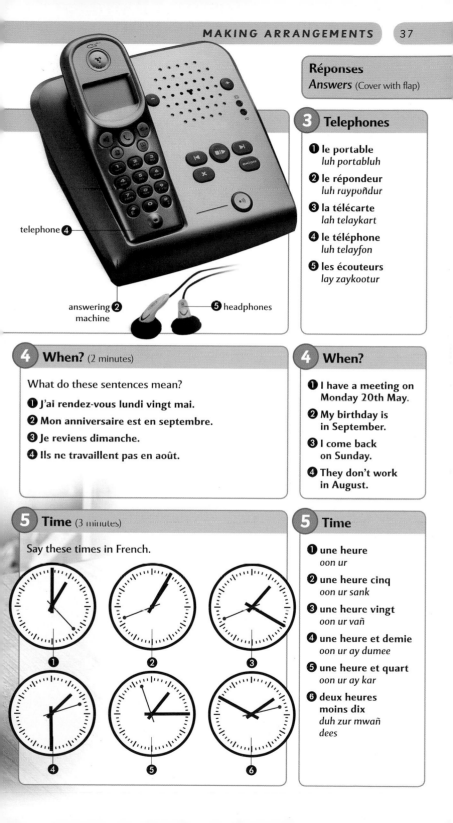

telephone ❹

answering ❷ machine

❺ headphones

3 Telephones

❶ **le portable**
luh portabluh

❷ **le répondeur**
luh raypoñdur

❸ **la télécarte**
lah telaykart

❹ **le téléphone**
luh telayfon

❺ **les écouteurs**
lay zaykootur

4 When? (2 minutes)

What do these sentences mean?

❶ J'ai rendez-vous lundi vingt mai.

❷ Mon anniversaire est en septembre.

❸ Je reviens dimanche.

❹ Ils ne travaillent pas en août.

4 When?

❶ I have a meeting on Monday 20th May.

❷ My birthday is in September.

❸ I come back on Sunday.

❹ They don't work in August.

5 Time (3 minutes)

Say these times in French.

❶ ❷ ❸ ❹ ❺ ❻

5 Time

❶ **une heure**
oon ur

❷ **une heure cinq**
oon ur sank

❸ **une heure vingt**
oon ur vañ

❹ **une heure et demie**
oon ur ay dumee

❺ **une heure et quart**
oon ur ay kar

❻ **deux heures moins dix**
duh zur mwañ dees

1 Warm up (1 minute)

Count to 100 in tens.
(pp.10-11, pp.30-1)

Ask "At what time?"
(pp.30-1)

Say "Half-past one".
(pp.30-1)

AU GUICHET
At the ticket office

In France, before getting on the train, you must *validate* (**composter**) your ticket by stamping it. Special orange machines are installed in every train station for this purpose. Fines are handed out to those who forget to validate their tickets. Most trains have both first and second class seats.

2 Words to remember (3 minutes)

Learn these words and then test yourself.

la gare *lah gar*	station
le train *luh trañ*	train
la voiture *lah vwatyur*	carriage
le billet *luh beeyay*	ticket
aller-simple *allay-sañpluh*	single
aller-retour *allay-rutoor*	return
première classe *prumyair klas*	first class
en seconde *oñ sugond*	second class

le passager
luh pasahjay
passenger

le quai
luh kay
platform

La gare est pleine de monde.
lah gar ay plen duh moñd
The station is crowded.

3 In conversation (4 minutes)

Deux billets pour Bordeaux s'il vous plaît.
duh beeyay poor bordoe seel voo play

Two tickets for Bordeaux, please.

Aller-retour?
allay rutoor

Return?

Oui. Je dois réserver des places?
wee. juh dwah rayzurvay day plas

Yes. Do I need to reserve seats?

4 Useful phrases (5 minutes)

Learn these phrases and then test yourself using the cover flap.

Le train pour Poitiers est annulé.
luh trañ poor pwatyer et anulay
The train for Poitiers is cancelled.

How much is a ticket to Lille?	**C'est combien un billet pour Lille?** *say koñbyañ uñ beeyay poor leel*
Do you accept credit cards?	**Vous acceptez les cartes de crédit?** *voo zakseptay lay kart duh kredee*
Do I have to change?	**Je dois changer?** *juh dwah shonjay*
Which platform does the train leave from?	**Le train part de quel quai?** *luh trañ par duh kel kay*
Are there discounts?	**Vous faites des réductions?** *voo fet day raydooksyoñ*
What time does the train for Paris leave?	**A quelle heure part le train pour Paris?** *ah kel ur par luh trañ poor paree*

5 Say it (2 minutes)

Which platform does the train for Paris leave from?

Three tickets to Lyon, please.

Cultural tip Most train stations now have automatic ticket machines that accept credit and debit cards as well as cash.

Ce n'est pas nécessaire. Quarante euros s'il vous plaît.
suh nay pah nesaysair. karont uroh seel voo play

That's not necessary. Forty euros please.

Vous acceptez les cartes de crédit?
voo zakseptay lay kart duh kredee

Do you accept credit cards?

Bien sûr. Le train part du quai numéro cinq.
byañ syur. luh trañ par doo kay noomairoe sank

Certainly. The train leaves from platform five.

ALLER ET PRENDRE
To go and to take

How do you say "train"? (pp.38-9)

What does "Le train part de quel quai?" mean? (pp.38-9)

Ask "When are you free?" (pp.32-3)

Aller (*to go*) and **prendre** (*to take*) are essential verbs in French. You can also use **prendre** to say *I'll have* (**je prends**) when you talk about food and drink. Note that the present tense in French includes the sense of a continuous action – for example, **je vais** means both *I go* and *I am going*.

2 **Aller: to go** (6 minutes)

Say the different forms of **aller** (*to go*) aloud. Use the flaps to test yourself and, when you are confident, practise the sample sentences below.

je vais *juh vay*	I go
tu vas *tew vah*	you go (informal singular)
il/elle va *eel/el vah*	he/she goes
nous allons *noo zalloñ*	we go
vous allez *voo zallay*	you go (formal singular or plural)
ils/elles vont *eel/el voñ*	they go

Où allez-vous? *oo allay voo*	Where are you going?
Je vais à Paris. *juh vay zah paree*	I'm going to Paris.
Nous allons à l'école en train. *noo zalloñ ah laykoloñ trañ*	We go to school by train.

Je vais à la Tour Eiffel.
juh vay zah lah toor eefel
I'm going to the Eiffel Tower.

Cultural tip The **TGV** (**train à grande vitesse**) is a fast train that can get you from Paris to the south of France in about three hours. Generally you will need to reserve a seat and can still choose smoking or non-smoking seats. **TER** (**trains express régionaux**) is another type of fast train. These trains are cheaper than the **TGV**. You can buy a ticket on the day of travel and get on without a reservation.

3 Prendre: to take (6 minutes)

Say the different forms of **prendre** (*to take*) aloud. Use the flaps to cover the French and test yourself. When you are confident, practise the sample sentences below.

je prends *juh proñ*	I take
tu prends *tew proñ*	you take (informal singular)
il/elle prend *eel/el proñ*	he/she takes
nous prenons *noo prunoñ*	we take
vous prenez *voo prunay*	you take (formal singular or plural)
ils/elles prennent *eel/el pren*	they take

Je prends le métro tous les jours.
juh proñ luh metroe too lay joor
I take the metro every day.

Je ne veux pas prendre un taxi. *juh nuh vuh pah proñdruh uñ taksee*	I don't want to take a taxi.
Prenez la première à gauche. *prunay lah prumyair ah gaush*	Take the first on the left.
Il prend le bœuf bourguignon. *eel proñ luh buf boorgheenyoñ*	He'll have the beef bourguignon.

4 Put into practice (2 minutes)

Cover the text on the right and complete the dialogue in French.

Où allez-vous? *oo allay voo*	**Je vais au Louvre.** *juh vay zoh loovruh*

Where are you going?

Say: I'm going to the Louvre.

Vous voulez prendre le métro? *voo voolay proñdruh luh metroe*	**Non, je veux aller en bus.** *noñ. juh vuh allay oñ boos*

Do you want to take the metro?

Say: No, I want to go by bus.

① **Warm up** (1 minute)

Say "I'd like to go to the station". (pp.40-1)

Ask "Where are you going?" (pp.40-1)

Say "fruit" and "cheese". (pp.24-5).

TAXI, BUS, ET MÉTRO
Taxi, bus, and metro

With buses, as with trains, you need to validate your ticket in a machine at the time of travel. For the metro, there's a standard fare and you can also buy a **carnet**, a book of 10 tickets. It's unusual to flag down a taxi in the street. You need to find one of the many taxi ranks and wait there.

② **Words to remember** (4 minutes)

Familiarize yourself with these words.

le bus *luh boos*	bus
le car *luh kar*	coach
la gare routière *lah gar rootyair*	bus station
l'arrêt de bus (m) *laray duh boos*	bus stop
le tarif *luh tareef*	fare
le taxi *luh taksee*	taxi
la rangée de taxis *lah roñjay duh taksee*	taxi rank
la station de métro *lah stasyoñ duh metroe*	metro station

Le bus numéro 4 s'arrête ici?
luh boos noomairoe katruh saret eesee
Does the number 4 bus stop here?

③ **In conversation: taxi** (2 minutes)

Le marché aux fromages, s'il vous plaît.
luh marshayoe fromarj, seel voo play

The cheese market, please.

Oui, sans problème, monsieur.
wee. soñ problem musyuh

Yes, no problem, sir.

Vous pouvez me déposer ici, s'il vous plaît?
voo poovay muh dayposay eesee, seel voo play

Can you drop me here, please?

4 Useful phrases (4 minutes)

Learn these phrases and then test yourself using the cover flap.

I want a taxi to the Arc de Triomphe.	**Je veux un taxi pour l'Arc de Triomphe.** *juh vuh uh taksee poor lark duh treeoñf*
When is the next bus to the station?	**Quand est le prochain bus pour la gare?** *koñ ay luh proshen boos poor lah gar*
How do you get to the museum?	**Pour aller au musée?** *poor allay oh moozay*
How long is the journey?	**Le trajet dure combien de temps?** *luh trajay dyur koñbyañ duh toñ*
Please wait for me.	**Attendez-moi s'il vous plaît.** *atonday-mwah seel voo play*

Cultural tip Métro lines (**lignes**) in Paris are known by the names of the first and last stations on the line. Follow the signs to the relevant end station – for example, direction Porte d'Orléans. Look out for the beautiful art deco Métropolitain signs retained in some stations.

6 Say it (2 minutes)

Do you go near the train station?

The fruit market, please.

When's the next coach to Calais?

5 In conversation: bus (2 minutes)

Vous allez près du musée?
vooz allay pray doo moozay

Do you go near the museum?

Oui. Ça fait quatre-vingt centimes.
wee. sah fay katruh vañ sonteem

Yes. That's 80 cents.

Dites-moi quand on arrive, s'il vous plaît.
deet mwah koñ toñ areev, seel voo play

Tell me when we arrive, please.

EN ROUTE
On the road

1 **Warm up** (1 minute)

How do you say "I have..."? (pp.14-15)

Say "my father", "my sister", and "my parents". (pp.16-17)

Say "I'm going to Paris". (pp.40-1)

Be sure to familiarize yourself with the French rules of the road before driving in France. French **autoroutes** (*motorways*) are fast but expensive. They are toll (**péage**) roads in which you usually take a ticket as you join the motorway and pay according to the distance travelled as you leave it.

2 **Match and repeat** (4 minutes)

Match the numbered items to the list on the left, then test yourself.

1 **le coffre**
luh kofrue

2 **le pare-brise**
luh parbreez

3 **le capot**
luh kapoh

4 **le pneu**
luh pnuh

5 **la roue**
lah roo

6 **la portière**
lah portyair

7 **le pare-chocs**
luh parshok

8 **les phares**
lay far

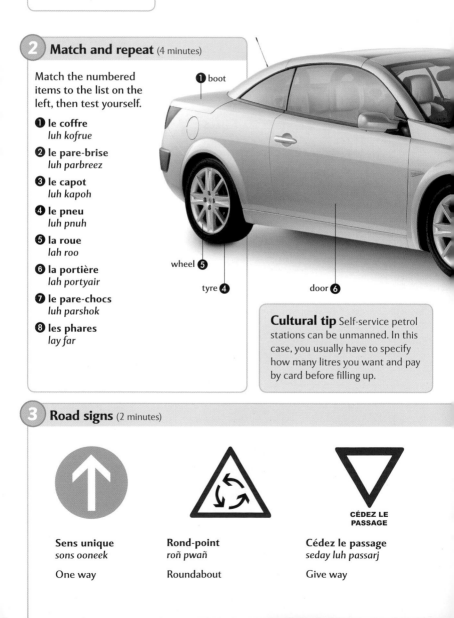

1 boot

wheel **5**

tyre **4**

door **6**

Cultural tip Self-service petrol stations can be unmanned. In this case, you usually have to specify how many litres you want and pay by card before filling up.

3 **Road signs** (2 minutes)

Sens unique
sons ooneek

One way

Rond-point
roñ pwañ

Roundabout

CÉDEZ LE PASSAGE

Cédez le passage
seday luh passarj

Give way

4 Useful phrases (4 minutes)

Learn these phrases and then test yourself using the cover flap.

My indicator doesn't work. **Mon clignotant ne marche pas.**
moñ kleenyoe-toñ nuh marsh pah

Fill it up, please **Le plein, s'il vous plaît.**
luh plañ, seel voo play

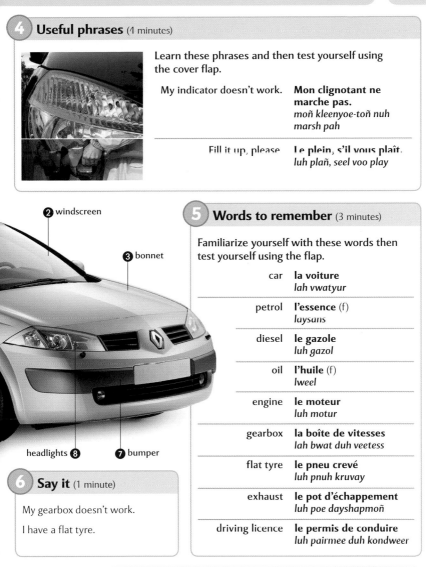

② windscreen

③ bonnet

headlights ⑧   ⑦ bumper

5 Words to remember (3 minutes)

Familiarize yourself with these words then test yourself using the flap.

car	**la voiture** *lah vwatyur*
petrol	**l'essence** (f) *laysans*
diesel	**le gazole** *luh gazol*
oil	**l'huile** (f) *lweel*
engine	**le moteur** *luh motur*
gearbox	**la boîte de vitesses** *lah bwat duh veetess*
flat tyre	**le pneu crevé** *luh pnuh kruvay*
exhaust	**le pot d'échappement** *luh poe dayshapmoñ*
driving licence	**le permis de conduire** *luh pairmee duh kondweer*

6 Say it (1 minute)

My gearbox doesn't work.

I have a flat tyre.

Passage protégé
passarj protayjay

Priority road

Sens interdit
sons añtairdee

No entry

Défense de stationner
dayfoñs duh stahseeonay

No parking

RÉVISEZ ET RÉPÉTEZ
Review and repeat

Réponses
Answers Cover with flap

1 Transport

❶ **le bus**
luh boos

❷ **le taxi**
luh taksee

❸ **la voiture**
lah vwatyur

❹ **le train**
luh trañ

❺ **le vélo**
luh vayloe

❻ **le métro**
luh metroe

1 Transport (3 minutes)

Name these forms of
transport in French.

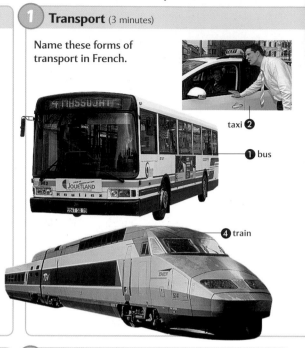

taxi ❷

❶ bus

❹ train

2 Go and take

❶ **allons**
alloñ

❷ **vais**
vay

❸ **prend**
proñ

❹ **allez**
allay

❺ **prenez**
prunay

❻ **prends**
proñ

2 Go and take (4 minutes)

Use the correct form of the
verb in brackets.

❶ Nous _____ à la Tour Eiffel. (aller)

❷ Je _____ à la gare. (aller)

❸ Elle _____ rendez-vous lundi. (prendre)

❹ Où _____-vous? (aller)

❺ Que _____ -vous? (prendre)

❻ Je _____ le bœuf. (prendre)

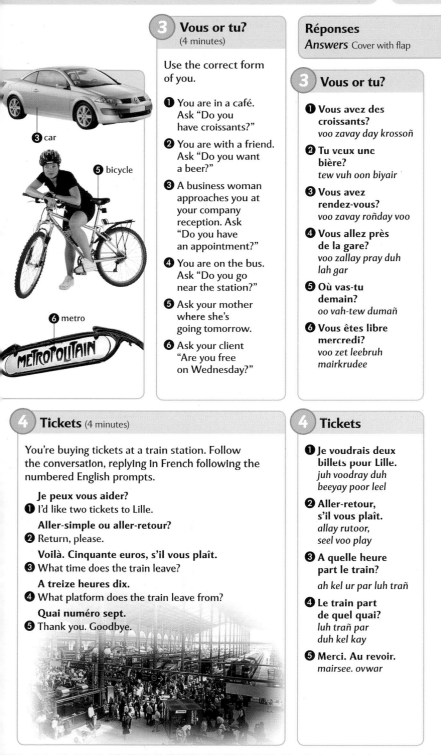

3 car

5 bicycle

6 metro

METROPOLITAIN

3 Vous or tu?
(4 minutes)

Use the correct form of you.

1 You are in a café. Ask "Do you have croissants?"

2 You are with a friend. Ask "Do you want a beer?"

3 A business woman approaches you at your company reception. Ask "Do you have an appointment?"

4 You are on the bus. Ask "Do you go near the station?"

5 Ask your mother where she's going tomorrow.

6 Ask your client "Are you free on Wednesday?"

Réponses
Answers Cover with flap

3 Vous or tu?

1 Vous avez des croissants?
voo zavay day krossoñ

2 Tu veux une bière?
tew vuh oon biyair

3 Vous avez rendez-vous?
voo zavay roñday voo

4 Vous allez près de la gare?
voo zallay pray duh lah gar

5 Où vas-tu demain?
oo vah-tew dumañ

6 Vous êtes libre mercredi?
voo zet leebruh mairkrudee

4 Tickets (4 minutes)

You're buying tickets at a train station. Follow the conversation, replying in French following the numbered English prompts.

Je peux vous aider?
1 I'd like two tickets to Lille.

Aller-simple ou aller-retour?
2 Return, please.

Voilà. Cinquante euros, s'il vous plaît.
3 What time does the train leave?

A treize heures dix.
4 What platform does the train leave from?

Quai numéro sept.
5 Thank you. Goodbye.

4 Tickets

1 Je voudrais deux billets pour Lille.
juh voodray duh beeyay poor leel

2 Aller-retour, s'il vous plaît.
allay rutoor, seel voo play

3 A quelle heure part le train?
ah kel ur par luh trañ

4 Le train part de quel quai?
luh trañ par duh kel kay

5 Merci. Au revoir.
mairsee. ovwar

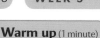

① Warm up (1 minute)

Ask "How do you get to the musuem?" (pp.42-3)

Say "I want to take the metro" and "I don't want to take a taxi". (pp.40-1)

EN VILLE
About town

Most French towns still have a market day and a thriving community of small shops. Even small villages usually have a mayor and a town hall. There may be parking restrictions in the town centre. Look out for signs for **parcmètres** (*pay and display*) and **défense de stationner** (*parking forbidden*).

② Match and repeat (4 minutes)

Match the numbered locations to the words in the panel.

❶ **la mairie**
lah mayree

❷ **le pont**
luh poñ

❸ **le centre ville**
luh sontruh veel

❹ **l'église** (f)
legleez

❺ **le parking**
luh parking

❻ **la place**
lah plas

❼ **la galerie d'art**
lah galree dar

❽ **le musée**
luh moozay

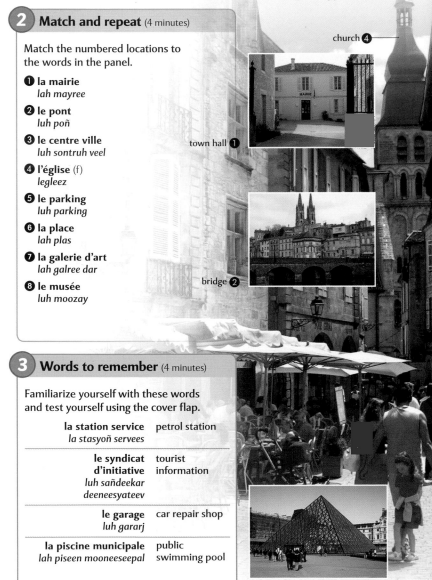

church ❹

town hall ❶

bridge ❷

③ Words to remember (4 minutes)

Familiarize yourself with these words and test yourself using the cover flap.

la station service *la stasyoñ servees*	petrol station
le syndicat d'initiative *luh sañdeekar deeneesyateev*	tourist information
le garage *luh gararj*	car repair shop
la piscine municipale *lah piseen mooneeseepal*	public swimming pool

❼ art gallery

4 Useful phrases (4 minutes)

La cathédrale est au centre-ville
lah kataydral et oh sontruh veel
The cathedral is in the town centre.

Learn these phrases and then test yourself using the cover flap.

Is there an art gallery in town?	**Il y a une galerie d'art en ville?** *eelyah oon galree dar oñ veel*
Is it far from here?	**C'est loin d'ici?** *say lwañ deesee*
There is a swimming pool near the bridge.	**Il y a une piscine près du pont.** *eelyah oon piseen pray doo poñ*
There isn't a library.	**Il n'y a pas de bibliothèque.** *eenyah pah duh bib-lee-yotek*

5 Put into practice (2 minutes)

Join in this conversation. Read the French on the left and follow the instructions to make your reply. Then test yourself by concealing the answers with the cover flap.

car park **5**

3 town centre

6 square

museum **8**

Je peux vous aider? *juh puh voo zeday*	**Il y a une bibliothèque en ville?** *eelyah oon bib-lee-yotek oñ veel*
Can I help you?	
Ask: Is there a library in town?	
Non, mais il y a un musée. *noñ may eelyah uñ moozay*	**Pour aller au musée?** *poor allay oh moozay*
No, but there's a museum.	
Ask: How do I get to the museum?	
C'est là-bas. *say lah bah*	**Merci beaucoup.** *mairsee bohkoo*
It's over there.	
Say: Thank you very much.	

1 Warm up (1 minute)

How do you say "near to the station"? (pp.42-3)

Say "Take the first on the left". (pp.40-1)

Ask "Where are you going?" (pp.40-1)

LES DIRECTIONS
Finding your way

To help you find your way, you'll often find a **plan de la ville** (*town plan*) situated in the town, usually near the town hall or tourist office. In the older parts of French towns there are often narrow streets, in which you will usually find a one-way system in operation. Parking is usually restricted.

2 Useful phrases (4 minutes)

Learn these phrases and then test yourself.

tournez à gauche/droite *toornay ah gaush/dwrat*	turn left/right
sur la gauche/droite *sewr lah gaush/dwrat*	on the right/left
tout droit *too dwrah*	straight on
Pour aller à la piscine? *poor allay ah lah piseen*	How do I get to the swimming pool?
la première à gauche *lah prumyair ah gaush*	first on the left
la deuxième à droite *lah duzyem ah dwrat*	second on the right

le marché couvert
luh marshay coovair
indoor market

la zone piétonne
lah zohn peeayton
pedestrian zone

Tournez à gauche à la grande place
toornay ah gaush ah lah groñd plas
Turn left at the main square.

3 In conversation (4 minutes)

Il y a un bon restaurant en ville?
eelyah uh boñ restoroñ oñ veel

Is there a good restaurant in town?

Oui, près de la gare.
wee, pray duh lah gar

Yes, near the station.

Pour aller à la gare?
poor allay ah lah gar

How do I get to the station?

4 Words to remember (4 minutes)

Je me suis perdue.
juh muh swee pairdoo
I'm lost.

Familiarize yourself with these words and test yourself using the cover flap.

traffic lights	**les feux** *lay fuh*
corner	**le coin** *luh kwañ*
street/road	**la rue** *lah roo*
main road	**la rue principale** *lah roo prañseepal*
at the end	**au bout** *oh boo*
map	**la carte** *lah kart*
cross over	**traversez** *travairsay*
opposite	**en face de** *oñ fass duh*

le monument
luh moonyumoñ
monument

le plan de la ville
luh plañ duh lah veel
town plan

5 Say it (2 minutes)

Turn right at the end of the street.

It's opposite the town hall.

It's ten minutes by bus.

Tournez à gauche aux feux et puis tout droit.
toornay ah gaush oh fuh ay pwee too dwrah

Turn left at the traffic lights and then straight on.

C'est loin?
say lwañ

Is it far?

Non, c'est cinq minutes à pied.
noñ, say sank minoot ah pyay

No, it's five minutes on foot.

LE TOURISME
Sightseeing

Say the days of the week in French. (pp.28-9)

How do you say "at six o'clock"? (pp.30-1)

Ask "What time is it?" (pp.30-1)

Most national museums close on Tuesdays and public holidays. Although shops are normally closed on Sundays, in tourist areas many will remain open all weekend. It is not unusual, particularly in rural areas, for shops and public buildings to close at lunch time.

2 **Words to remember** (4 minutes)

Familiarize yourself with these words and test yourself using the flap.

le guide *luh geed*	guide book
l'entrée (f) *loñtray*	entrance ticket
les heures d'ouverture (f) *lay zur doovairtyur*	opening times
le jour férié *luh joor fairiyay*	public holiday
l'entrée gratuite (f) *loñtray gratweet*	free entrance

la visite guidée
lah viseet geeday
guided tour

Cultural tip The majority of public buildings and private offices close for public holidays. Many public and private offices are closed in August. If a public holiday falls on a Thursday, the French will often **faire le pont** (*do the bridge*) - in other words, take Friday off as well to make a long weekend.

3 **In conversation** (3 minutes)

Vous ouvrez cet après-midi?
voo zoovray set apray-meedee

Do you open this afternoon?

Oui, mais nous fermons à quatre heures.
wee, may noo fairmoñ ah katruh

Yes, but we close at four o'clock.

Vous avez un accès pour les fauteuils roulants?
voo zavay uñ aksay poor lay fohtuhee roolañ

Do you have wheelchair access?

4 Useful phrases (3 minutes)

Learn these phrases and then test yourself using the cover flap.

What time do you open/close?	**Vous ouvrez/fermez à quelle heure?** *voo zoovray/fairmay ah kel ur*
Where are the toilets?	**Où sont les toilettes?** *oo soñ lay twalet*
Is there wheelchair access?	**Il y a un accès pour les fauteuils roulants?** *eelyah uñ aksay poor lay fohtuhee roolañ*

5 Put into practice (4 minutes)

Cover the text on the right and complete the dialogue in French.

Désolé. Le musée est fermé.
dezoluy. luh moozay ay fairmay

Sorry. The museum is closed.

Vous ouvrez le mardi?
voo zoovray luh mardee

Ask: Do you open on Tuesdays?

Oui, mais nous fermons tôt.
wee, may noo fairmoñ toe

Yes, but we close early.

A quelle heure?
ah kel ur

Ask: At what time?

Oui, il y a un ascenseur là-bas.
wee, eelyah uñ asoñsur lah-bah

Yes, there's a lift over there.

Merci, je voudrais quatre entrées.
mairsee, juh voodray katruh oñtray.

Thank you, I'd like four entrance tickets.

Voilà, et le guide est gratuit.
vwalah, ay luh geed ay gratwee

Here you are, and the guidebook is free.

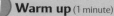

1 Warm up (1 minute)

Say "You're on time".
(pp.14-15)

What's the French for
"ticket"? (pp.38-9)

Say "I am going to
New York". (pp.40-1)

A L'AÉROPORT
At the airport

Although the airport environment is largely universal, it is sometimes useful to be able to ask your way around the terminal in French. It's a good idea to make sure you have a few one-euro coins when you arrive at the airport; you may need to pay for a baggage trolley.

2 Words to remember (4 minutes)

l'enregistrement (m) *loñrejeestrumoñ*	check-in
le départ *luh depar*	departures
l'arrivée (f) *lareevay*	arrivals
la douane *lah doo-an*	customs
le contrôle des passeports *luh kontrol day passpor*	passport control
le terminal *luh termee-nal*	terminal
la porte d'embarquement *lah port doñbarkumoñ*	gate
le numéro de vol *luh noomairoe duh vol*	flight number

Familiarize yourself with these words and test yourself using the flap.

Quelle est la porte d'embarquement pour le vol numéro vingt-trois?
kel ay lah port doñbarkumoñ poor luh vol numairoh vañ-trwah
What gate does flight 23 leave from?

3 Useful phrases (3 minutes)

Learn these phrases and then test yourself using the cover flap.

Le vol pour Nice est à l'heure? *luh vol poor nees et ah lur*	Is the flight for Nice on time?

Je ne trouve pas mes bagages. *juh nuh troov pah may bagarj*	I can't find my baggage.

Le vol pour Londres est retardé. *luh vol poor londruh ay retarday*	The flight to London is delayed.

4 Put into practice (3 minutes)

Join in this conversation. Read the French on the left and follow the instructions to make your reply. Then test yourself by concealing the answers with the cover flap.

Bonsoir, monsieur. Je peux vous aider?
boñswar, musyuh. juh puh voo zayday

Good evening, sir. Can I help you?

Ask: Is the flight to Paris on time?

Le vol pour Paris est à l'heure?
luh vol poor paree et ah lur

Oui, monsieur
wee musyuh

Yes, sir.

Ask: What gate does it leave from?

Quelle est la porte d'embarquement?
kel ay lah port doñbarkumoñ

5 Match and repeat (4 minutes)

Match the numbered items to the French words in the panel.

❶ la carte d'embarquement
lah kart doñbarkumoñ

❷ l'enregistrement des bagages (m)
loñrejeestrumoñ day bagarj

❸ le billet
luh beeyay

❹ le passeport
luh passpor

❺ la valise
lah valeez

❻ le bagage à main
luh bagarj ah mañ

❼ le chariot
luh shareeyoh

boarding ❶ pass

baggage ❷ check-in

ticket ❸

passport ❹

❼ trolley

❺ suitcase   ❻ hand luggage

Réponses
Answers (Cover with flap)

RÉVISEZ ET RÉPÉTEZ
Review and repeat

1 Places

❶ le musée
luh moozay

❷ la mairie
lah mayree

❸ le pont
luh poñ

❹ la galerie d'art
lah galree dar

❺ le parking
luh parking

❻ la cathédrale
lah kataydral

❼ la place
lah plas

1 Places (4 minutes)

Name the numbered places in French.

❶ museum ❷ town hall ❸ bridge

❹ art gallery ❺ car park

❻ cathedral

❼ square

2 Car parts

❶ le pare-brise
luh parbreez

❷ le clignotant
luh kleenyoe-toñ

❸ le capot
luh kapoh

❹ le pneu
luh pnuh

❺ la portière
lah portyair

❻ le pare-chocs
luh parshok

2 Car parts (3 minutes)

Name these car parts in French.

windscreen ❶

❹ tyre ❺ door

3 **Questions** (4 minutes)

Ask the questions that match these answers.

❶ **Le car part à huit heures.**
luh kar par ah weet ur

❷ **Le café, c'est deux euros cinquante.**
luh kafay, say duh zuroh sankont

❸ **Non, je ne veux pas de vin.**
noñ. juh nuh vuh pah duh vañ

❹ **Le train part du quai cinq.**
luh trañ par doo kay sank

❺ **Nous allons à Paris.**
noo zalloñ ah paree

❻ **Non, c'est cinq minutes à pied.**
noñ, say sank minoot ah pyay

3 **Questions**

❶ **Le car part à quelle heure?**
luh kar par ah kel ur

❷ **C'est combien le café?**
say koñbyañ luh kafay

❸ **Vous voulez du vin?**
voo voolay doo vañ

❹ **Le train part de quel quai?**
luh trañ par duh kel kay

❺ **Où allez-vous?**
oo allay voo

❻ **C'est loin?**
say lwañ

❷ indicator

❸ bonnet

❻ bumper

4 **Verbs** (4 minutes)

Choose the correct words to fill the gaps.

❶ Je _____ anglais.

❷ Nous _____ le bus.

❸ Elle _____ à Paris.

❹ Il _____ trois filles.

❺ Tu _____ un thé?

❻ Combien d'enfants _____ -vous?

❼ Je _____ rendez-vous pour mardi.

❽ Où _____ les toilettes?

4 **Verbs**

❶ **suis**
swee

❷ **prenons**
prunoñ

❸ **va**
vah

❹ **a**
ah

❺ **veux**
vuh

❻ **avez**
avay

❼ **prends**
proñ

❽ **sont**
soñ

RÉSERVER LES CHAMBRES
Booking a room

How do you ask in French "Do you accept credit cards?" (pp.38–9)

Ask "How much is that?" (pp.18-19)

Ask "Do you have children?" (pp.12-13)

There are different types of accommodation: **l'hôtel,** categorized from one to five stars; **la pension,** a small family-run hotel; and **les chambres d'hôte** (like bed and breakfast) which are often situated in beautiful old properties.

2 **Useful phrases** (3 minutes)

Practise these phrases and then test yourself by concealing the French on the left with the cover flap.

Le petit-déjeuner est compris?
luh puhtee dayjunay ay koñpree

Is breakfast included?

Vous acceptez les animaux de compagnie?
voo zakseptay lay zanimoe duh koñpañee

Do you accept pets?

Vous avez un room service?
voo zavay uñ room survees

Do you have room service?

Il faut libérer la chambre à quelle heure?
eel foe leeburay lah shombruh ah kel ur

What time do I have to vacate the room?

3 **In conversation** (5 minutes)

Vous avez des chambres libres?
voo zavay day shombruh leebruh

Do you have any vacancies?

Oui, une chambre double.
wee, oon shombruh doobluh

Yes, a double room.

Vous avez un lit d'enfant?
voo zavay uñ lee doñfoñ

Do you have a cot?

4 Words to remember (4 minutes)

Familiarize yourself with these words and test yourself by concealing the French on the right with the cover flap.

La chambre donne sur le jardin?
lah shombruh don syur luh jardañ
Does the room have a view over the garden?

room	**la chambre** *lah shombruh*
single room	**la chambre simple** *lah shombruh sampluh*
double room	**la chambre double** *lah shombruh doobluh*
twin room	**la chambre twin** *lah shombruh twin*
bathroom	**la salle de bains** *lah sal duh bañ*
shower	**la douche** *lah doosh*
breakfast	**le petit-déjeuner** *luh puhtee dayjunay*
key	**la clé** *lah klay*
balcony	**le balcon** *luh bulkoñ*
air conditioning	**la climatisation** *lah kleematee-zasyoñ*

5 Say it (2 minutes)

Do you have a single room?

Does the room have a balcony?

Cultural tip Chambres d'hôte are usually the only type of accommodation to include breakfast in the price of the room. In other types of hotel you will usually be charged extra. Many two- or three-star hotels belong to the Logis de France association, which guarantees standards of accommodation and service.

Pas de problème. Combien de nuits?
pah duh prob-lem. koñbyañ duh nwee

No problem. How many nights?

Pour trois nuits.
poor trwah nwee

For three nights.

Très bien. Voici la clé.
tray byañ. vwasee lah klay

Very good. Here's the key.

A L'HÔTEL
In the hotel

1 Warm up (1 minute)

How do you say "is there...?" and "there isn't..."? (pp.48-9)

What does "Je peux vous aider?" mean? (pp.48-9)

Although the larger hotels almost always have bathrooms en suite, there are still some **pensions** and **chambres d'hôte** with shared facilities. This can also be the case in some economy hotels, where a whole family can stay the night for less than the price of a tank of petrol.

2 Match and repeat (6 minutes)

Match the numbered items in this hotel bedroom with the French text in the panel and test yourself using the cover flap.

❶ **la table de chevet**
lah tabluh duh shuvay

❷ **la lampe**
lah lomp

❸ **la stéréo**
lah stairayoe

❹ **les rideaux** (m)
lay reedoe

❺ **le canapé**
luh kanapay

❻ **l'oreiller** (m)
lorayay

❼ **le coussin**
luh koosañ

❽ **le lit**
luh lee

❾ **le dessus de lit**
luh dusoo duh lee

❿ **la couverture**
lah coovurtyur

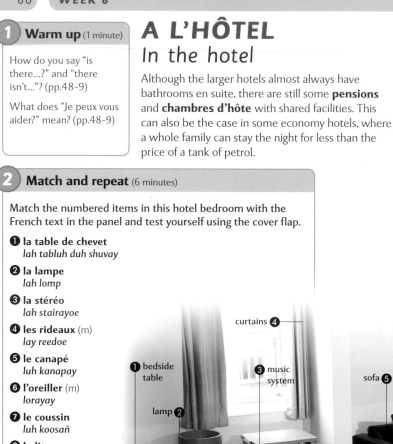

❹ curtains

❶ bedside table

❸ music system

sofa ❺

lamp ❷

❻ pillow   ❼ cushion   ❽ bed   ❾ bedspread   ❿ blanket

Cultural tip When you arrive in your room, you will usually see a long sausage-shaped pillow on the bed called **le traversin** - nowadays a largely decorative item. These are hard and not very comfortable. However, you can usually find square, softer pillows (**les oreillers**) in the cupboard. Do not hesitate to ask if you can't find any.

3 Useful phrases (5 minutes)

Familiarize yourself with these phrases and then test yourself.

The room is too cold/hot.	**La chambre est trop froide/chaude.** *lah shombruh ay troe fwrard/shohd*
There are no towels.	**Il n'y a pas de serviettes.** *eenyah pah duh survyet*
I need some soap.	**J'ai besoin de savon.** *jay buzwañ duh savoñ*
The shower doesn't work very well.	**La douche ne marche pas très bien.** *lah doosh nuh marsh pah tray byañ*
The lift has broken down.	**L'ascenseur est en panne.** *lasohsur ay toñ pan*

4 Put into practice (3 minutes)

Cover the text on the right and complete the dialogue in French.

Je peux vous aider?
juh puh voo zayday

Can I help you?

Say: I need some pillows.

J'ai besoin d'oreillers.
jay buzwañ dorayay

La femme de chambre va les apporter.
la fam duh shambruh vah lay zaportay

The maid will bring some.

Say: And the television doesn't work.

Et la télévision ne marche pas.
ay lah telayveesyoñ nuh marsh pah

1 Warm up (1 minute)

Ask "Can I?" (pp.34–5)

What is French for "the shower"? (pp.60–1)

Say "I need some towels". (pp.60–1)

AU CAMPING
At the campsite

Camping is popular in France and there are many well-organized campsites. These are rated by a star system. Most towns have **un camping municipal** (*public campsite*), and there are also many private sites. Campfires are usually forbidden, but you can often hire a barbecue.

2 Useful phrases (3 minutes)

Familiarize yourself with these phrases and then test yourself using the cover flap.

Je peux louer un vélo? *juh puh looway uñ vayloe*	Can I rent a bicycle?
C'est de l'eau potable? *say duh loe potabluh*	Is this drinking water?
Les feux de camp sont permis? *lay fuh duh koñ soñ pairmee*	Are campfires allowed?
Les radios sont interdites. *lay radyo soñ añtairdeet*	Radios are forbidden.

Le camping est tranquille
luh komping ay troñkeel
The campsite is quiet.

le bureau du camping
luh buroh doo komping
campsite office

la poubelle
lah poobel
litter bin

le double toit
luh doobluh twah
fly sheet

3 In conversation: (5 minutes)

J'ai besoin d'un emplacement pour trois nuits.
jay buzwañ d'uñ oñplasmoñ poor trwah nwee

I need a pitch for three nights.

Il y en a un près de la piscine.
eelyon ah uñ pray duh lah piseen

There's one near the swimming pool.

C'est combien pour une caravane?
say koñbyañ poor oon karavan

How much is it for a caravan?

5 Say it (2 minutes)

I need a pitch for four nights.

Can I rent a tent?

Where's the electrical hook-up?

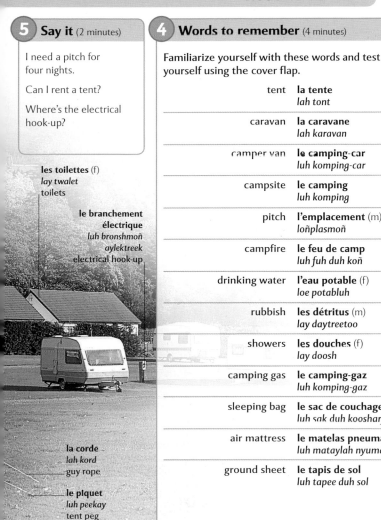

les toilettes (f)
lay twalet
toilets

le branchement électrique
luh bronshmoñ aylektreek
electrical hook-up

la corde
lah kord
guy rope

le piquet
luh peekay
tent peg

4 Words to remember (4 minutes)

Familiarize yourself with these words and test yourself using the cover flap.

tent	**la tente** *lah tont*
caravan	**la caravane** *lah karavan*
camper van	**le camping-car** *luh komping-car*
campsite	**le camping** *luh komping*
pitch	**l'emplacement** (m) *loñplasmoñ*
campfire	**le feu de camp** *luh fuh duh koñ*
drinking water	**l'eau potable** (f) *loe potabluh*
rubbish	**les détritus** (m) *lay daytreetoo*
showers	**les douches** (f) *lay doosh*
camping gas	**le camping-gaz** *luh komping-gaz*
sleeping bag	**le sac de couchage** *luh sak duh koosharj*
air mattress	**le matelas pneumatique** *luh mataylah nyumateek*
ground sheet	**le tapis de sol** *luh tapee duh sol*

Cinquante euros, avec une nuit d'avance.
sankoñt uroh, avek oon nwee davons

Fifty euros, one night in advance.

Je peux louer un barbecue?
juh puh looway uñ barbekyoo

Can I rent a barbecue?

Oui, mais vous devez verser des arrhes.
wee, may voo duvay vairsay day zar

Yes, but you must pay a deposit.

LES DESCRIPTIONS
Descriptions

1 Warm up (1 minute)

Say "hot" and "cold".
(pp.60-1)

What is the French for
"bathroom" (pp.58-9),
"bed", and "pillow"?
(pp.60-1)

Adjectives are words used to describe people, things, and places. In French you generally put the adjective after the thing it describes - for example, **une chambre froide** (*a cold room*), but in some cases the adjective is placed before - for example, **un grand café** (*a large coffee*).

2 Words to remember (7 minutes)

Adjectives can change slightly depending on whether the thing described is masculine (**le**), feminine (**la**), or plural (**les**), but often this affects only the spelling, not the pronunciation. Below, the masculine spelling is followed by the feminine. For the plural form, just add a (silent) "s" to the appropriate masculine or feminine form.

grand/grande *groñ/groñd*	big/tall
petit/petite *puhtee/puhteet*	small
chaud/chaude *shoh/shohd*	hot
froid/froide *fwrah/fwrad*	cold
bon/bonne *boñ/bon*	good
mauvais/mauvaise *movay/movez*	bad
lent/lente *loñ/lont*	slow
rapide/rapide *rapeed/rapeed*	fast
bruyant/bruyante *breeyoñ/breeyont*	noisy
tranquille/tranquille *troñkeel/troñkeel*	quiet
dur/dure *dyuh/dyuh*	hard
mou/molle *moo/moll*	soft
beau/belle *boe/bell*	beautiful
laid/laide *leh/led*	ugly

la haute montagne
lah oht moñtanhyuh
high mountain

la basse colline
lah bas koleen
low hill

la petite maison
lah puhteet mayzon
small house

la vieille église
lah veeyay egleez
old church

Le village est très beau.
luh veelarj ay tray boe
The village is very beautiful.

3 Useful phrases (4 minutes)

You can emphasize a description by using **très** (*very*), **trop** (*too*), or **plus** (*more*) before the adjective.

This coffee is cold.	**Ce café est froid.** *suh kafay ay fwrah*
My room is very noisy.	**Ma chambre est très bruyante.** *mah shombruh ay tray breeyont*
My car is too small.	**Ma voiture est trop petite.** *mah vwatyur ay troe puhteet*
I need a softer bed.	**J'ai besoin d'un lit plus mou.** *jay buzwañ d'uñ lee ploo moo*

4 Put into practice (3 minutes)

Join in this conversation. Cover up the text on the right and complete the dialogue in French. Check and repeat if necessary.

Voici la chambre. *vwasee lah shombruh* Here is the bedroom. Say: The view is very beautiful.	**La vue est très belle.** *lah voo ay tray bell*
La salle de bains est là-bas. *luh sal duh bañ ay lah-bah* The bathroom is over there. Say: It is too small.	**Elle est trop petite.** *el ay troe puhteet*
Nous n'en avons pas d'autre. *noo nañavoñ pah dotruh* We haven't got another. Say: Then we'll take the room.	**Alors nous prenons la chambre.** *Alor noo prunoñ lah shombruh*

Réponses
Answers (Cover with flap)

RÉVISEZ ET RÉPÉTEZ
Review and repeat

1 Adjectives

❶ **chaude**
shohd

❷ **mou**
moo

❸ **bon**
boñ

❹ **petite**
puhteet

❺ **tranquille**
troñkeel

1 Adjectives (3 minutes)

Put the adjective in brackets into French, using the correct masculine or feminine form.

❶ La chambre est trop _____ . (hot)

❷ Je voudrais un oreiller plus _____ . (soft)

❸ Le café est _____ . (good)

❹ Cette salle de bains est trop _____ . (small)

❺ Vous avez une chambre plus _____ ? (quiet)

2 Campsite

❶ **le branchement électrique**
luh bronshmoñ aylektreek

❷ **la tente**
lah tont

❸ **la poubelle**
lah poobel

❹ **la corde**
lah kord

❺ **les toilettes**
lay twalet

❻ **la caravane**
lah karavan

2 Campsite (3 minutes)

Name these items you might find in a campsite.

tent ❷

guy rope ❹

electrical ❶
hook-up

litter bin ❸

3 At the hotel (4 minutes)

You are booking a room in a hotel. Follow the conversation, replying in French by following the English prompts.

Je peux vous aider?
❶ Do you have any vacancies?

Oui, une chambre double.
❷ Do you accept pets?

**Oui. C'est pour
combien de nuits?**
❸ Three nights.

Ça fait deux cent quarante euros.
❹ Is breakfast included?

**Bien sûr,
voici la clé.**
❺ Thank you
very much.

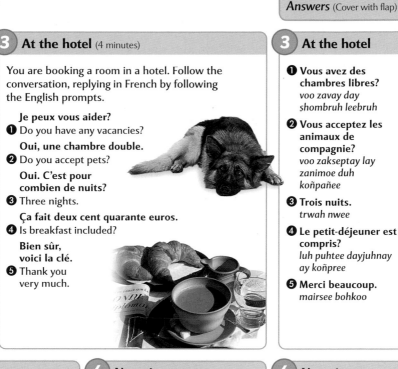

3 At the hotel

❶ **Vous avez des
chambres libres?**
*voo zavay day
shombruh leebruh*

❷ **Vous acceptez les
animaux de
compagnie?**
*voo zakseptay lay
zanimoe duh
koñpañee*

❸ **Trois nuits.**
trwah nwee

❹ **Le petit-déjeuner est
compris?**
*luh puhtee dayjuhnay
ay koñpree*

❺ **Merci beaucoup.**
mairsee bohkoo

4 Negatives (5 minutes)

Make these sentences negative using the verb in brackets.

❶ Je _____ d'enfants.
(avoir)

❷ Elle _____ à Paris demain.
(aller)

❸ Il _____ de vin.
(vouloir)

❹ Je _____ le train pour Nice.
(prendre)

❺ Le café _____ chaud. (être)

❺ toilets

❻ caravan

4 Negatives

❶ **n'ai pas**
nay pah

❷ **ne va pas**
nuh vah pah

❸ **ne veut pas**
nuh vuh pah

❹ **ne prends pas**
nuh proñ pah

❺ **n'est pas**
nay pah

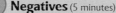

LES MAGASINS
Shops

1 **Warm up** (1 minute)

Ask "How do I get to the station?" (pp.50-1)

Say "Turn left at the traffic lights", "Cross over the street", "The station is opposite the café". (pp.50-1)

In town centres, shops (**magasins**) are often traditional, specialist outlets. But you can also find big supermarkets and shopping malls on the outskirts of major towns. Local markets selling fresh, local produce can be found everywhere. You can find out the market day at the tourist office.

2 **Match and repeat** (5 minutes)

Match the numbered shops below and right to the French in the panel. Then test yourself using the cover flap.

1 **la boulangerie**
lah booloñjuree

2 **la pâtisserie**
lah pateesree

3 **le tabac**
luh tabah

4 **la boucherie**
lah boosheree

5 **la charcuterie**
lah sharkooterie

6 **la librairie**
lah leebrairee

7 **la poissonnerie**
lah pwasoñree

8 **l'épicerie** (m)
laypeesree

9 **la banque**
lah boñk

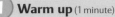

1 baker

2 cake shop

4 butcher

5 delicatessen

7 fishmonger

8 grocer

Cultural tip As well as supplying medicines and health products, a French pharmacy (**pharmacie**) will sell expensive perfume and cosmetics but not generally an everyday bar of soap or a tube of toothpaste. The latter are found at the supermarket or general store. The **tabac** (*tobacconist*) is the place for newspapers and stamps, but also often incorporates a café and bar.

Où est la fleuriste?
oo ay lah flureest
Where is the florist?

3 tobacconist

6 bookshop

9 bank

5 **Say it** (2 minutes)

Where is the bank?

Do you sell cheese?

Where do I pay?

3 **Words to remember** (4 minutes)

Familiarize yourself with these words and test yourself using the flap.

hardware shop	**la quincaillerie** *lah kañkayeree*
antique shop	**l'antiquaire** (m) *lañteekair*
hairdresser	**le coiffeur** *luh kwafur*
jeweller	**la bijouterie** *lah bee-jooteree*
post office	**la poste** *lah post*
shoemaker	**la cordonnerie** *lah kordoneree*
dry cleaner	**le pressing** *luh praysing*
confectioner	**le confiseur** *luh koñfeesur*
cheese shop	**la fromagerie** *lah fromajeree*

4 **Useful phrases** (3 minutes)

Familiarize yourself with these phrases.

Where is the hairdresser?	**Où est le coiffeur?** *oo ay luh kwafur*
Where do I pay?	**Je dois payer où?** *juh dwah payay oo*
I'm just looking, thank you.	**Je regarde, merci.** *juh rugard, mairsee*
Do you sell phonecards?	**Vous vendez des télécartes?** *voo vonday day telaykart*
I'd like two of these.	**J'en veux deux.** *joñ vuh duh*
Is there a department store in town?	**Il y a un grand magasin en ville?** *eelyah uñ groñ magazañ oñ veel*
Can I place an order?	**Je peux passer une commande?** *juh puh passay oon komond*

AU MARCHÉ
At the market

1 **Warm up** (1 minute)

What is French for 40, 56, 77, 82, and 94? (pp.30-1)

Say "I'd like a big room". (pp.64-5)

Ask "Do you have a small car?" (pp.64-5)

France uses the metric system of weights and measures. You need to ask for produce in kilogrammes or grammes. You may find that the older generation still use the term **une livre** (*a pound*) meaning half a kilo. Some larger items such as melons are sold individually **à la pièce**.

2 **Match and repeat** (4 minutes)

Match the numbered items in this scene with the text in the panel.

1 **les courgettes** (f)
lay korjet

2 **la salade**
lah sah-lad

3 **les citrons** (m)
lay sitroñ

4 **les poireaux** (m)
lay pwaroe

5 **les tomates** (f)
lay toemat

6 **les champignons** (m)
lay shoñpeeyoñ

7 **les avocats** (m)
lay zavokah

8 **les pommes de terre** (f)
lay pom duh tair

courgettes **1**

tomatoes **5**   **6** mushrooms   **8** potatoes

avocados **7**

3 **In conversation** (3 minutes)

Je voudrais des tomates.
juh voodray day toemat

I'd like some tomatoes.

Des grosses ou des petites?
day gros oo day puhteet

The large ones or the small ones?

Deux kilos de grosse, s'il vous plaît.
duh keeloe duh gros, seel voo play

Two kilos of the large ones, please.

Cultural tip France now uses the common European currency, the euro. This is divided into 100 cents, which the French call **centimes** after the old divisions of the franc. You will usually hear the price given as: **dix euros**, **vingt** (€10.20), **six euros**, **soixante-treize** (€6.73), etc.

❷ lettuce

❸ lemons

❹ leeks

4 Useful phrases (5 minutes)

Learn these phrases. Then cover up the answers on the right. Read the English under the pictures and say the phrase in French as shown on the right.

Le fromage de chèvre est trop cher.
luh fromarj duh shevruh ay troe shair

The goat's cheese is too expensive.

C'est combien ce fromage?
say koñbyañ suh fromarj

How much is that cheese?

5 Say it (2 minutes)

Three kilos of potatoes, please.

The mushrooms are too expensive.

How much is the lettuce?

Ce sera tout.
suh surah too

That'll be all.

Et avec ceci, madame.
ay avek susee, ma-dam

Anything else, madam.

Ce sera tout, merci. C'est combien?
suh surah too, mairsee. say koñbyañ

That'll be all, thank you. How much?

Trois euros, cinquante.
trwah zuroh, sankont

Three euros, fifty.

AU SUPERMARCHÉ
At the supermarket

1 Warm up (1 minute)

What are these items you could buy in a supermarket (pp.24-5)?

la viande
le poisson
le fromage
le jus de fruits
le vin
l'eau

Prices in supermarkets are usually lower than in smaller shops. They offer all kinds of products, with the larger out-of-town **hypermarchés** (*hypermarkets*) extending to clothes, household goods, garden furniture, and DIY products. They may also stock regional products.

2 Match and repeat (5 minutes)

Look at the numbered items and match them to the French words in the panel on the left.

❶ **les produits d'entretien** (m)
lay prodwee doñtruh-tiañ

❷ **les fruits** (m)
lay froo-wee

❸ **les boissons** (m)
lay bwassoñ

❹ **les plats préparés** (m)
lay plah prayparay

❺ **les légumes** (m)
lay laygoom

❻ **les produits surgelés** (m)
lay prodwee surjulay

❼ **les produits laitiers** (m)
lay prodwee letyay

❽ **les produits de beauté** (m)
lay prodwee duh boetay

household products ❶

fruit ❷

drinks ❸

ready meals ❹

vegetables ❺

frozen foods ❻

Cultural tip Fruit and vegetables sold by the kilo are usually weighed and priced at a separate counter. Alternatively, there may sometimes be a self-service weighing machine.

3 Useful phrases (3 minutes)

Learn these phrases and then test yourself using the cover flap.

May I have a bag, please?	**Je peux avoir un sac, s'il vous plaît?** _juh puh avwar uñ sak, seel voo play_
Where is the drinks aisle?	**Où est le rayon des boissons?** _oo ay luh rayonn day bwassoñ_
Where is the check-out, please?	**Où est la caisse, s'il vous plaît?** _oo ay lah kes, seel voo play_
Please key in your pin.	**Tapez votre code, s'il vous plaît.** _tapay votruh kod, seel voo play_

8 beauty products

7 dairy products

4 Words to remember (4 minutes)

Learn these words and then test yourself using the cover flap.

bread	**le pain** _luh pañ_
milk	**le lait** _luh lay_
butter	**le beurre** _luh bur_
ham	**le jambon** _luh joñboñ_
salt	**le sel** _luh sel_
pepper	**le poivre** _luh pwavruh_
washing powder	**la lessive** _lah leseev_
toilet paper	**le papier toilette** _luh papyay twalet_
nappies	**les couches** (f) _lay koosh_
washing-up liquid	**le liquide vaisselle** _luh likeed vaysel_

5 Say it (2 minutes)

Where's the dairy products aisle?

May I have some ham, please?

Where are the frozen foods?

1 Warm up (1 minute)

Say "I'd like…". (pp.22-3)

Ask "Do you have…? (pp.14-5)

Say "38", "42", and "46". (pp.30-1)

Say "large", "small", "bigger", and "smaller". (pp.64-5)

VÊTEMENTS ET CHAUSSURES
Clothes and shoes

Clothes and shoes are measured in metric sizes. Even allowing for conversion of sizes, French clothes tend to be cut smaller than English ones. Note that clothes size is **la taille** but shoe size is **la pointure**.

2 Match and repeat (3 minutes)

Match the numbered items of clothing to the French words in the panel on the left. Use the cover flap to test yourself.

❶ la chemise
lah shumeez

❷ la cravate
lah kravat

❸ la veste
lah vest

❹ la poche
lah posh

❺ la manche
lah moñsh

❻ le pantalon
luh poñtaloñ

❼ la jupe
lah joop

❽ le collants (m)
luh kolloñ

❾ les chaussures (f)
lay shohsyur

shirt ❶

tie ❷

jacket ❸

pocket ❹

sleeve ❺

trousers ❻

Cultural tip Like most of Europe, France uses the continental system of sizes. Dress sizes usually range from 36 (UK 8, US 6) through to 46 (UK 20, US 18) and shoe sizes from 37 (UK 4½, US 6) to 45 (UK 11, US 12). For men's shirts, a size 41 is a 16-inch collar, 43 is a 17-inch collar, and 45 is an 18-inch collar.

3 Useful phrases (5 minutes)

Learn these phrases and then test yourself using the cover flap.

Do you have a larger size?	**Vous avez une taille plus grande?** *voo zavay oon tie ploo groñd*
It's not what I want.	**Ce n'est pas ce que je veux.** *suh nay pah sukuh juh vuh*
I'll take the pink one.	**Je prends la rose.** *juh proñ lah roz*

4 Words to remember (4 minutes)

Colours are adjectives (pp.64–5) and often have a masculine, feminine, and plural form. The feminine is usually formed by adding an **e** and the plural by adding an **s**.

red	**rouge/rouge** *rooj/rooj*
white	**blanc/blanche** *bloñ/blonsh*
blue	**bleu/bleue** *bluh/bluh*
yellow	**jaune/jaune** *jon/jon*
green	**vert/verte** *vair/vairt*
black	**noir/noire** *nwar/nwar*

7 skirt

8 tights

9 shoes

5 Say it (2 minutes)

I'll take the yellow one.

Do you have this jacket in black?

I'd like a 38.

Do you have a smaller size?

RÉVISEZ ET RÉPÉTEZ
Review and repeat

1 Market

❶ **les tomates**
lay toemat

❷ **les champignons**
lay shoñpeeyoñ

❸ **les pommes de terre**
lay pom duh tair

❹ **les courgettes**
lay korjet

❺ **la salade**
lah sah-lad

❻ **les avocats**
lay zavokah

1 Market (3 minutes)

Name the numbered vegetables in French.

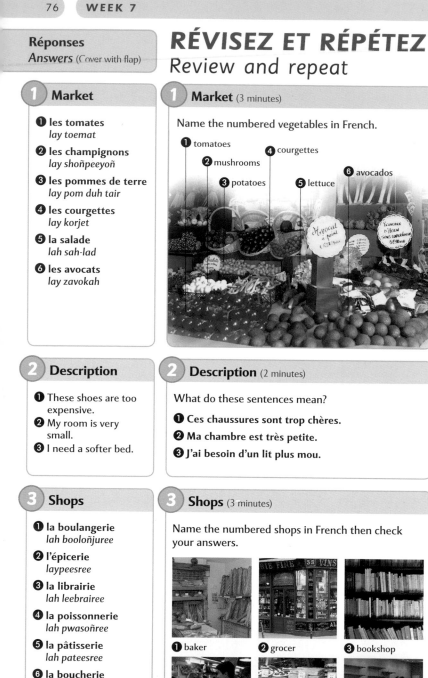

❶ tomatoes
❷ mushrooms
❸ potatoes
❹ courgettes
❺ lettuce
❻ avocados

2 Description

❶ These shoes are too expensive.
❷ My room is very small.
❸ I need a softer bed.

2 Description (2 minutes)

What do these sentences mean?

❶ Ces chaussures sont trop chères.
❷ Ma chambre est très petite.
❸ J'ai besoin d'un lit plus mou.

3 Shops

❶ **la boulangerie**
lah booloñjuree

❷ **l'épicerie**
laypeesree

❸ **la librairie**
lah leebrairee

❹ **la poissonnerie**
lah pwasoñree

❺ **la pâtisserie**
lah pateesree

❻ **la boucherie**
lah boosheree

3 Shops (3 minutes)

Name the numbered shops in French then check your answers.

❶ baker
❷ grocer
❸ bookshop
❹ fishmonger
❺ cake shop
❻ butcher

4 Supermarket (3 minutes)

What is the French for the numbered product categories?

① household products

② beauty products

③ drinks

④ dairy products

⑤ frozen foods

4 Supermarket

① **les produits d'entretien**
lay prodwee doñtruh-tiañ

② **les produits de beauté**
lay prodwee duh boetay

③ **les boissons**
lay bwassoñ

④ **les produits laitiers**
lay prodwee letyay

⑤ **les produits surgelés**
lay prodwee surjulay

5 Museum (4 minutes)

Follow this conversation replying in French following the English prompts.

Bonjour. Je peux vous aider?
① Three adults and two children.

Ça fait soixante-dix euros.
② That's very expensive!

Nous ne faisons pas de réductions pour les enfants.
③ How much is a guide?

Quinze euros.
④ Five tickets and a guide, please.

Quatre-vingt-cinq euros, s'il vous plaît.
⑤ Here you are. Where are the toilets?

Là-bas.
⑥ Thank you very much.

5 Museum

① **Trois adultes et deux enfants.**
trwah zadoolt ay duh zoñfoñ

② **C'est très cher!**
say tray shair

③ **C'est combien pour un guide?**
say koñbyañ poor uñ geed

④ **Cinq entrées et un guide, s'il vous plaît**
sank oñtray ay tuñ geed, seel voo play

⑤ **Voilà. Où sont les toilettes?**
vwalah. oo soñ lay twalet

⑥ **Merci beaucoup.**
mairsee bohkoo

1 Warm up (1 minute)

Ask "which platform?" (pp.38-9)

What is the French for the following family members: "sister", "brother", "mother", "father", "son", and "daughter"? (pp.10-11)

OCCUPATIONS
Jobs

Some occupations have a different form when the person is female - for example, **infirmier** (*male nurse*) and **infirmière** (*female nurse*). Others such as **professeur** remain the same for men and women. When you say your occupation, you don't use **un/une** (*a*); as in **Je suis avocat** (*I'm a lawyer*).

2 Words to remember: jobs (7 minutes)

Familiarize yourself with these occupations and test yourself using the flap. The feminine form is shown in parentheses.

médecin *medsañ*	doctor
dentiste *doñteest*	dentist
infirmier(ière) *añfairmyay(yair)*	nurse
professeur *profesur*	teacher
comptable *koñtabluh*	accountant
avocat(e) *avokah(aht)*	lawyer
designer *deesienur*	designer
consultant(e) *koñsooltoñ(oñt)*	consultant
secrétaire *sekraytair*	secretary
commerçant(e) *komairsoñ(oñt)*	shopkeeper
électricien(ne) *aylektreesyañ(en)*	electrician
plombier *ploñbyay*	plumber
cuisinier(ière) *kweeseenyay(yair)*	cook/chef
ingénieur *añjaynyur*	engineer
à mon compte *ah moñ kont*	self-employed

Je suis plombier.
juh swee ploñbyay
I'm a plumber.

Elle est professeur.
el ay profesur
She is a teacher.

3 Put into practice (4 minutes)

Join in the conversation. Conceal the text on the right with the cover flap and complete the dialogue in French.

Quelle est votre profession? *kel ay votruh profesyoñ*	**Je suis consultant.** *juh swee koñsooltoñ*
What do you do?	
Say: I am a consultant.	

Vous travaillez pour quelle compagnie? *voo trav-eyeyay poor kel koñpanee*	**Je suis à mon compte.** *juh swee ah moñ kont*
What company do you work for?	
Say: I'm self-employed.	

Comme c'est intéressant! *kom say añtayraysoñ*	**Et quelle est votre profession?** *ay kel ay votruh profesyoñ*
How interesting!	
Ask: What is your profession?	

Je suis dentiste. *juh swee doñteest*	**Ma sœur est dentiste aussi.** *mah sur ay doñteest ohsee*
I'm a dentist.	
Say: My sister is a dentist too.	

4 Words to remember: workplace (3 minutes)

Familiarize yourself with these words and test yourself.

Le siège social est à Lille.
lluh syej sosyal ay tah leel
Head office is in Lille.

head office	**le siège social** *luh syej sosyal*
branch	**lah succursale** *lah sookoorsal*
department	**le département** *luh daypartumoñ*
reception	**la réception** *lah resepsyoñ*
manager	**le chef** *luh shef*
trainee	**le stagiaire** *luh stajyair*

1 **Warm up** (1 minute)

Practise different ways of introducing yourself in different situations (pp.8-9). Mention your name, occupation, nationality, and any other information you'd like to volunteer.

LE BUREAU
The office

An office environment or business situation has its own vocabulary in any language, but there are many items for which the terminology is virtually universal. Be aware that French computer keyboards have a different layout to the standard English QWERTY convention.

2 **Words to remember** (5 minutes)

Familiarize yourself with these words. Read them aloud several times and try to memorize them. Conceal the French with the cover flap and test yourself.

le moniteur *luh moneetur*	monitor
l'ordinateur (m) *lordeenatur*	computer
la souris *lah sooree*	mouse
l'email (m) *leemail*	e-mail
l'internet (m) *lañtairnet*	internet
le mot de passe *luh moh duh pas*	password
la messagerie téléphonique *lah mesah-juree telayfoneek*	voicemail
le fax *luh fax*	fax machine
le copieur *luh kopee-ur*	photocopier
l'agenda (m) *lajeñdah*	diary
la carte de visite *lah kart duh veezeet*	business card
la réunion *lah rayoonyon*	meeting
la conférence *lah konfayroñs*	conference
l'ordre du jour (m) *lordruh doo joor*	agenda

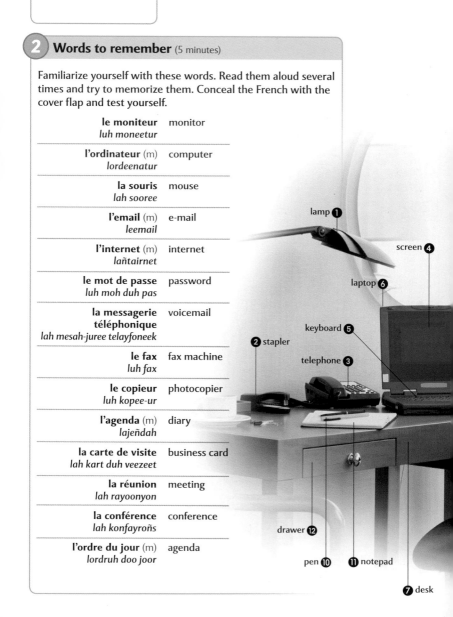

lamp **1**

screen **4**

laptop **6**

2 stapler

keyboard **5**

telephone **3**

drawer **12**

pen **10**   **11** notepad

7 desk

3 Useful phrases (2 minutes)

Learn these phrases and then test yourself using the cover flap.

I need to make some photocopies.	**J'ai besoin de faire des photocopies.** *jay buzwañ duh fair day fotokopee*
I'd like to arrange an appointment.	**Je voudrais prendre rendez-vous.** *juh voodray proñdruh roñday-voo*
I want to send an e-mail.	**Je veux envoyer un email.** *juh vuh oñvwayay uñ eemail*

4 Match and repeat (5 minutes)

Match the numbered items to the French words on the right.

5 Say it (2 minutes)

I'd like to arrange a conference.

I need to send a fax.

Do you have a laptop?

clock **8**

printer **9**

13 swivel chair

1 **la lampe**
lah lomp

2 **l'agrafeuse** (f)
lagrafurz

3 **le téléphone**
luh telayfon

4 **l'écran** (m)
laykroñ

5 **le clavier**
luh klaveeyay

6 **l'ordinateur portable** (m)
lordeenatur portabluh

7 **le bureau**
luh byuroh

8 **la pendule**
lah poñdool

9 **l'imprimante** (f)
lampreemont

10 **le stylo**
el luh steeloh

11 **le bloc-notes**
eluh blok-not

12 **le tiroir**
luh teerwar

13 **la chaise tournante**
lah shayz toornont

LE MONDE ACADÉMIQUE
Academic world

1 Warm up (1 minute)

Say "How interesting!" (p.78-9), "library" (pp.48-9), and "traffic lights". (pp.50-1)

Ask "What is your profession?" and answer "I'm an engineer". (pp.78-9)

In France **une licence** (*batchelor's degree*) generally takes three years, followed by **une maîtrise** (*master's degree*) and **un doctorat** (*PhD*). Paris has several universities, often referred to by Roman numerals, as in Paris V.

2 Useful phrases (3 minutes)

Familiarize yourself with these phrases and then test yourself.

Quel est votre secteur? *kel ay votruh sektur*	What is your field?
Je fais de la recherche en chimie. *juh fay duh lah reshairsh oñ sheemee*	I am doing research in chemistry.
J'ai une licence en droit. *jay oon leesons oñ dwrah*	I have a degree in law.
Je fais une présentation sur l'architecture moderne. *juh fay oon praysoñtasyoñ syur larsheetektur modairn*	I am giving a presentation on modern architecture.

3 In conversation (5 minutes)

Bonjour, je suis professeur Stein.
boñjoor, juh swee profesur stayeen

Hello, I'm Professor Stein.

De quelle université êtes-vous?
duh kel ooneevair-sitay et voo

What university are you from?

Je suis déléguée de l'université Paris II.
juh swee daylaygay duh looneevair-sitay paree duh

I'm the delegate from Paris II University.

4 Words to remember (4 minutes)

Familiarize yourself with these words and then test yourself.

Nous avons un stand à la foire-exposition.
noo zavon uñ stond ah lah fwar ekspohseesyoñ
We have a stand at the trade fair.

5 Say it (2 minutes)

I'm doing research in medicine.

I have a degree in literature.

She's the professor.

conference	**la conférence** *lah koñfayroñs*
trade fair	**la foire-exposition** *lah fwar-ekspohseesyoñ*
seminar	**le séminaire** *luh semeenair*
lecture theatre	**l'amphithéâtre** (m) *loñfeetayatruh*
conference room	**la salle de conférences** *lah sal duh koñfayroñs*
exhibition	**l'exposition** (f) *lekspohzeesyoñ*
library	**la bibliothèque** *lah biblee-yotek*
university lecturer	**le maître de conférences** *luh metruh duh koñfayroñs*
professor	**le professeur** *luh profesur*
medicine	**la médecine** *lah medseen*
science	**la science** *lah siyons*
literature	**la littérature** *lah leetairatyur*
engineering	**l'ingénierie** (f) *lahjayneeuree*

Quel est votre secteur?
kel ay votruh sektur

What's your field?

Je fais de la recherche en ingénierie.
juh fay duh lah reshairsh oñ lahjayneeuree

I'm doing research in engineering.

Comme c'est intéressant.
kom say añtayraysoñ

How interesting.

LES AFFAIRES
In business

Ask "Can I ...?" (pp.34–5)

Say "I want to send an e-mail". (pp.80–1)

Ask "Can you send an e-mail?" (pp.80–1)

You will receive a more friendly reception and make a good impression if you make the effort to begin a meeting with a short introduction in French, even if your vocabulary is limited. After that, all parties will probably be happy to continue the meeting in English.

2 **Words to remember** (6 minutes)

On signe le contrat?
oñ seenuh luh koñtrah
Shall we sign the contract?

Familiarize yourself with these words and then test yourself by concealing the French with the cover flap.

le planning *luh planning*	schedule
la livraison *lah leevraysoñ*	delivery
le paiement *luh paymoñ*	payment
le budget *luh bujay*	budget
le prix *luh pree*	price
le document *luh dokoomoñ*	document
la facture *lah faktyur*	invoice
le devis *luh duhvees*	estimate
les bénéfices (m) *lay baynayfees*	profits
les ventes (f) *lay vont*	sales
les chiffres (m) *lay sheefruh*	figures

le client
luh kleeyoñ
client

Cultural tip In general, commercial dealings are formal, but a lunch with wine is still part of doing business in France. As a client, you can expect to be taken out to a restaurant and as a supplier you should consider entertaining your customers.

3 Useful phrases (6 minutes)

Memorize these phrases. Note that when asking *what...?* you use **quel(s)** with masculine words but **quelle(s)** with feminine words.

le contrat
luh koñtrah
contract

le cadre
luh kadruh
executive

Envoyez-moi le contrat s'il vous plaît.
oñvwayay mwah luh koñtrah, seel voo play

Please send me the contract.

Nous sommes convenus d'un planning?
noo som koñvunoo duñ planning

Have we agreed a schedule?

Quand pouvez-vous faire la livraison?
koñ poovay voo fair lah leevraysoñ

When can you make the delivery?

Quel est le budget?
kel ay luh bujay

What's the budget?

le rapport
luh rapor
report

Vous pouvez m'envoyer la facture?
voo poovay moñvwayay lah faktyur

Can you send me the invoice?

4 Say it (2 minutes)

Can you send me the estimate?

Have we agreed a price?

What are the profits?

RÉVISEZ ET RÉPÉTEZ
Review and repeat

1 At the office

❶ **l'agraffeuse**
lagrafurz

❷ **la lampe**
lah lomp

❸ **l'ordinateur portable**
lordeenatur portabluh

❹ **le stylo**
luh steeloh

❺ **le bureau**
luh byuroh

❻ **le bloc-notes**
luh blok-not

❼ **la pendule**
lah poñdool

1 At the office (4 minutes)

Name these items.

lamp ❷ ❸ laptop

pen ❹

clock ❼

stapler ❶

❺ desk   ❻ notepad

2 Jobs

❶ **médecin**
medsañ

❷ **plombier**
ploñbyay

❸ **commerçant**
comairsoñ(oñt)

❹ **comptable**
koñtabluh

❺ **professeur**
profesur

❻ **avocat**
avokah(aht)

2 Jobs (3 minutes)

What are these jobs in French?

❶ doctor

❷ plumber

❸ shopkeeper

❹ accountant

❺ teacher

❻ lawyer

3 Work (4 minutes)

Answer these questions following the English prompts.

Vous travaillez pour quelle compagnie?
❶ Say "I work for myself".

De quelle université êtes-vous?
❷ Say "I'm at the University of Bordeaux".

Quel est votre secteur?
❸ Say "I'm doing medical research".

Nous sommes convenus d'un planning?
❹ Say "Yes. Can you send me the budget?"

3 Work

❶ Je suis à mon compte.
juh swee zah moñ koñt

❷ Je suis de l'université de Bordeaux.
juh swee duh looneevair-sitay duh bordoe

❸ Je fais de la recherche en médecine.
juh fay duh lah reshairsh oñ medseen

❹ Oui. Vous pouvez m'envoyer le budget?
wee. voo poovay moñvwayay lah bujay

4 How much? (4 minutes)

Answer the question with the amount shown in brackets.

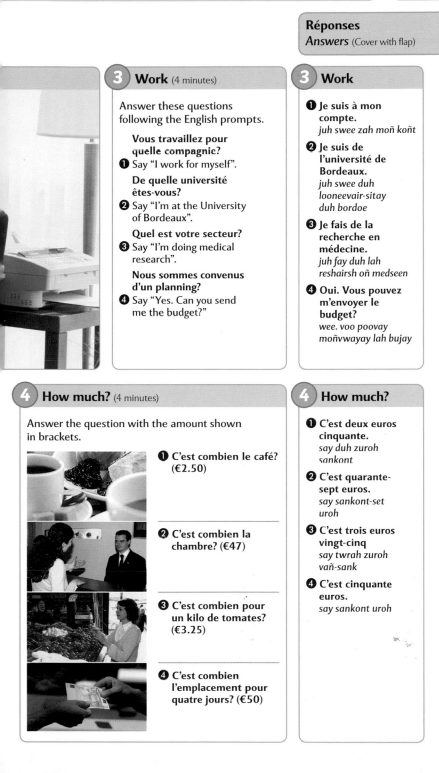

❶ C'est combien le café? (€2.50)

❷ C'est combien la chambre? (€47)

❸ C'est combien pour un kilo de tomates? (€3.25)

❹ C'est combien l'emplacement pour quatre jours? (€50)

4 How much?

❶ C'est deux euros cinquante.
say duh zuroh sankont

❷ C'est quarante-sept euros.
say sankont-set uroh

❸ C'est trois euros vingt-cinq
say twrah zuroh vañ-sank

❹ C'est cinquante euros.
say sankont uroh

1 Warm up (1 minute)

Say "I'm allergic to nuts".
(pp.24-5)

Say the verb "avoir" (to
have) in all its forms (je,
tu, il/elle, vous, nous, ils/
elles). (pp.14-5)

A LA PHARMACIE
At the chemist

French pharmacists study for seven years before
qualifying. They can give advice about minor
health problems and are permitted to dispense a
wide variety of medicines, even giving injections,
if necessary. There is a duty pharmacist
(**pharmacie de garde**) in most towns.

2 Match and repeat (3 minutes)

Match the numbered items to the French
words in the panel on the left and test
yourself using the flap.

❶ **le bandage**
luh boñdarj

❷ **le sirop**
luh seeroe

❸ **les gouttes** (f)
lay goot

❹ **le pansement**
luh poñsumoñ

❺ **la seringue**
lah surañg

❻ **la crème**
lah krem

❼ **le suppositoire**
luh soopozitwar

❽ **le cachet**
luh kashay

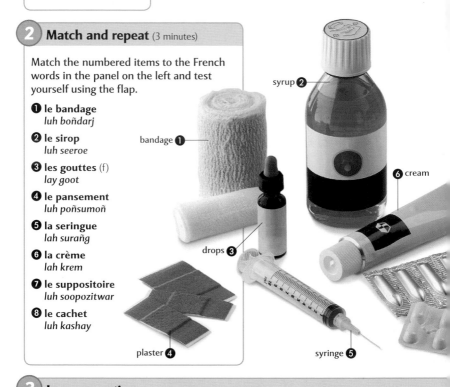

syrup ❷

bandage ❶

❻ cream

drops ❸

plaster ❹

syringe ❺

3 In conversation (3 minutes)

**Bonjour madame,
vous désirez?**
*boñjoor, mad-dam.
voo dayzeeray*

Hello madam. What
would you like?

J'ai mal à l'estomac.
jay mal ah lestomah

I have a stomach ache.

Vous avez la diarrhée?
voo zavay lah dyaray

Do you have diarrhoea?

4 Words to remember (2 minutes)

Familiarize yourself with these words and test yourself using the flap.

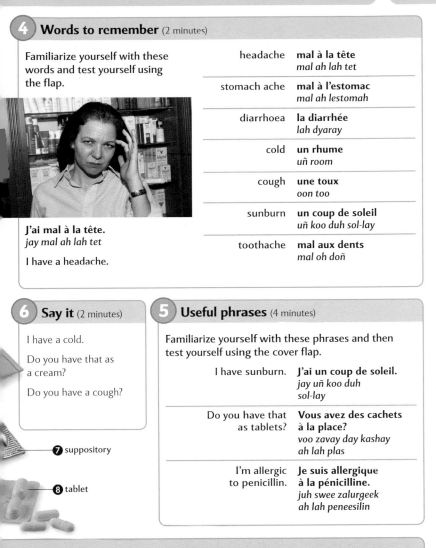

J'ai mal à la tête.
jay mal ah lah tet

I have a headache.

headache	**mal à la tête** *mal ah lah tet*
stomach ache	**mal à l'estomac** *mal ah lestomah*
diarrhoea	**la diarrhée** *lah dyaray*
cold	**un rhume** *uñ room*
cough	**une toux** *oon too*
sunburn	**un coup de soleil** *uñ koo duh sol-lay*
toothache	**mal aux dents** *mal oh doñ*

6 Say it (2 minutes)

I have a cold.

Do you have that as a cream?

Do you have a cough?

❼ suppository

❽ tablet

5 Useful phrases (4 minutes)

Familiarize yourself with these phrases and then test yourself using the cover flap.

I have sunburn.	**J'ai un coup de soleil.** *jay uñ koo duh sol-lay*
Do you have that as tablets?	**Vous avez des cachets à la place?** *voo zavay day kashay ah lah plas*
I'm allergic to penicillin.	**Je suis allergique à la pénicilline.** *juh swee zalurgeek ah lah peneesilin*

Non, mais j'ai aussi mal à la tête.
noñ, may jay osee mal ah lah tet

No, but I also have a headache.

Prenez ça.
prunay sah

Take this.

Vous avez un sirop à la place?
voo zavay uh seeroe ah lah plas

Do you have that as a syrup?

Say " I have a toothache" and "I have sunburn". (pp.88-9)

Say the French for "red", "green", "black", and "yellow". (pp.74-5)

LE CORPS
The body

The most common phrase for talking about aches and pains is **J'ai mal à**... Don't forget that when **à** is placed in front of **le** it becomes **au** and in front of **les** it becomes **aux** (the **x** is silent). For example, **J'ai mal au dos** (*I have a backache*) and **J'ai mal aux oreilles** (*I have earache*).

2 **Match and repeat: body** (6 minutes)

Match the numbered parts of the body with the list on the left. Test yourself by using the cover flap.

1 **la main**
lah mañ

2 **la tête**
lah tet

3 **l'épaule** (f)
laypoll

4 **le coude**
luh kood

5 **les cheveux**
lay shuhvuh

6 **le bras**
luh brah

7 **le cou**
luh koo

8 **la poitrine**
lah pwatreen

9 **l'estomac** (m)
lestomah

10 **la jambe**
lah jomb

11 **le genou**
luh juhnoo

12 **le pied**
luh piyay

1 hand
4 elbow
5 hair
2 head
shoulder **3**
6 arm
7 neck
chest **8**
stomach **9**
leg **10**
knee **11**
12 foot

3 Match and repeat: face (3 minutes)

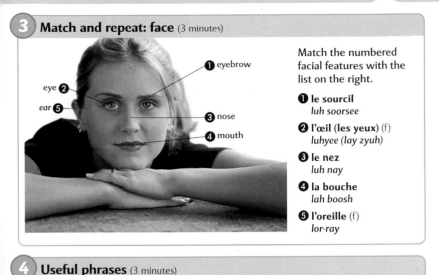

1 eyebrow

eye **2**

ear **5**

3 nose

4 mouth

Match the numbered facial features with the list on the right.

1 **le sourcil**
luh soorsee

2 **l'œil (les yeux)** (f)
luhyee (lay zyuh)

3 **le nez**
luh nay

4 **la bouche**
lah boosh

5 **l'oreille** (f)
lor-ray

4 Useful phrases (3 minutes)

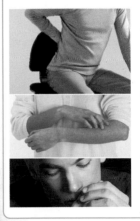

Learn these phrases and then test yourself using the cover flap.

I have a pain in my back. **J'ai une douleur au dos.** *jay oon doolur oe doh*

I have a rash on my arm. **J'ai une rougeur au bras.** *jay oon roojur oe brah*

I don't feel well. **Je ne me sens pas bien.** *juh nuh muh soñ pah byañ*

5 Put into practice (2 minutes)

Join in this conversation and test yourself using the cover flap.

Qu'est ce qui ne va pas? *keskee nuh vah pah*

What's the matter?

Say: I don't feel well.

Je ne me sens pas bien. *juh nuh muh soñ pah byañ*

Tu as mal où? *tew ah mal oo*

Where does it hurt?

Say: I have a pain in my shoulder.

J'ai une douleur à l'épaule. *jay oon doolur ah laypoll*

1 Warm up (1 minute)

Say "I need some tablets" and "He needs some cream". (pp.60-1 and pp.88-9)

What is the French for "I don't have a son"? (pp.10-15)

CHEZ LE DOCTEUR
At the doctor

Unless it's an emergency, you have to book an appointment with the doctor and pay when you leave. You can usually reclaim the money if you have medical insurance. You can find the names and addresses of local doctors from the local town hall or **syndicat d'initiative** (*tourist office*).

2 Useful phrases you may hear (3 minutes)

Familiarize yourself with these phrases and then test yourself using the cover flap to conceal the French on the left.

Ce n'est pas sérieux. *suh nay pah seryuh*	It's not serious.
Vous avez besoin de tests. *voo zavay buzwañ duh test*	You need to have tests.
Vous avez une infection aux reins. *voo zavay oon añfeksyoñ oh rañ*	You have a kidney infection.
Vous avez besoin d'aller à l'hôpital. *voo zavay buzwañ dalay ah lopeetal*	You need to go to hospital.

Vous prenez des médicaments?
 voo prunay day maydikamoñ
 Are you taking any medications?

3 In conversation (5 minutes)

Qu'est-ce qui ne va pas?
 keskee nuh vah pah

What's the matter?

J'ai une douleur à la poitrine.
 jay oon doolur ah lah pwatreen

I have a pain in my chest.

Laissez-moi vous examiner.
 lessay-mwah voo zekzaminay

Let me examine you.

4 Useful phrases you may need to say (4 minutes)

Je suis enceinte.
juh swee zoñsant
I'm pregnant.

Practise these phrases and then test yourself using the cover flap.

I'm diabetic.	**Je suis diabétique.** *juh swee diyabeteek*
I'm epileptic.	**Je suis épileptique.** *juh swee zepeelepteek*
I'm asthmatic.	**Je suis asthmatique.** *juh swee zasmateek*
I have a heart condition.	**J'ai un problème au cœur.** *jay uñ prob-lem oh kur*
I feel faint.	**Je vais m'évanouir.** *juh vay mayvanooweer*
I have a fever.	**J'ai de la fièvre.** *jay duh lah fyevruh*
It's urgent.	**C'est urgent.** *say turjoñ*

Cultural tip
If you are an EU national, you are entitled to free emergency medical treatment in France on production of a European Health Insurance Card or E111 form. For an ambulance call 112.

5 Say it (2 minutes)

Do I need tests?

My son needs to go to hospital.

It's not urgent.

C'est sérieux?
say seryuh

Is it serious?

Non, vous avez seulement une indigestion.
noñ, voo zavay surlmoñ oon añdeejestyoñ

No, you only have indigestion.

Quel soulagement!
kel soolarjemoñ

What a relief!

1 Warm up (1 minute)

Ask "How long is the journey?" (pp.42-3)

How do you ask "Do I need...?" (pp.92-3)

What is the French for "mouth" and "head"? (pp.90-1)

A L'HÔPITAL
At the hospital

The main hospitals in France are attached to universities and are known as **Centres Hospitaliers Universitaires** (CHU). It is useful to know a few basic phrases relating to hospitals for use in an emergency or in case you need to visit a friend or colleague in hospital.

2 Useful phrases (5 minutes)

Familiarize yourself with these phrases. Conceal the French with the cover flap and test yourself.

Quelles sont les heures de visite? *kel soñ lay zur duh vizeet*	What are the visiting hours?
Ça va prendre combien de temps? *sah vah prondruh koñbyañ duh toñ*	How long will it take?
Ça va faire mal? *sah vah fair mal*	Will it hurt?
Allongez-vous ici, s'il vous plaît. *aloñjay voo zeesee, seel voo play*	Please lie down here.
Vous ne devez pas manger. *voo nuh duvay pah moñjay*	You must not eat.
Ne bougez pas la tête. *nuh boojay pah lah tet*	Don't move your head.
Ouvrez la bouche, s'il vous plaît. *oovray lah boosh, seel voo play*	Please open your mouth.
Vous avez besoin d'une prise de sang. *voo zavay buzwañ doon preez duh soñ*	You need a blood test.

Où est la salle d'attente?
oo ay lah sal datont
Where is the waiting room?

l'intraveineuse (f)
lañtravaynurz
intravenous drip

Ça va mieux?
sah vah meeyuh
Are you feeling better?

3 Words to remember (4 minutes)

Memorize these words and test yourself using the cover flap.

emergency department	**la salle des urgences** *lah sal day zurjoñs*
children's ward	**le service de pédiatrie** *luh survees duh paydyah-tree*
operating theatre	**la salle d'opération** *lah sal dopairasyoñ*
x-ray department	**la salle de radiologie** *lah sal duh radyo-lojee*
waiting room	**la salle d'attente** *lah sal datont*
lift	**l'ascenseur** *lasoñsur*
stairs	**les escaliers** *lay zeskalyay*

Votre radio est normale.
votruh radyoh ay normal
Your x-ray is normal.

4 Put into practice (3 minutes)

Join in this conversation. Read the French on the left and follow the instructions to make your reply. Then test yourself by concealing the answers with the cover flap.

Vous avez une infection.
voo zavay oon añfeksyoñ

You have an infection.

Ask: Do I need tests?

J'ai besoin de tests?
jay buzwañ duh test

Tout d'abord, vous avez besoin d'une prise de sang.
too dabor, voo zavay buzwañ doon preez duh soñ

First you will need a blood test.

Ask: Will it hurt?

Ça va faire mal?
sah vah fair mal

5 Say it (2 minutes)

Does he need a blood test?

Where is the children's ward?

Do I need an x-ray?

Non, ne vous inquiétez pas.
noñ, nuh voo zañkyatay pah

No. Don't worry.

Ask: How long will it take?

Ça va prendre combien de temps?
sah vah prondruh koñbyañ duh toñ

Réponses
Answers (Cover with flap)

RÉVISEZ ET RÉPÉTEZ
Review and repeat

1 The body

1 la tête
lah tet

2 le bras
luh brah

3 la poitrine
lah pwatreen

4 l'estomac
lestomah

5 la jambe
lah jomb

6 le genou
luh juhnoo

7 le pied
luh piyay

1 The body (4 minutes)

Name the numbered
body parts in French.

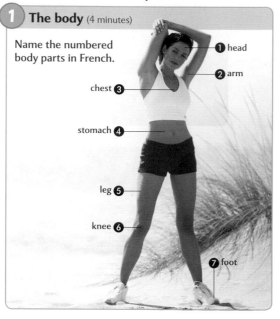

1 head
2 arm
chest **3**
stomach **4**
leg **5**
knee **6**
7 foot

2 On the phone

1 Je voudrais parler à
Caroline Martin.
*juh voodray parlay ah
karoleen martañ*

2 [your name] de
l'imprimerie
Laporte.
*[your name] duh
lahpreemuree laport*

3 Je peux laisser
un message?
*juh puh laysay
uñ mesarj*

4 C'est bon pour le
rendez-vous lundi à
onze heures.
*say boñ poor luh
roñday-voo lañdee
ah onz ur*

5 Merci, au revoir.
mairsee, ovwar

2 On the phone (4 minutes)

You are arranging an appointment. Follow the
conversation, replying in French following
the English prompts.

Allô, société Apex.
1 I'd like to speak to
Caroline Martin.

**Oui, c'est de la part
de qui?**
2 [your name] of Laporte
printers.

**Je suis désolé, la ligne
est occupée.**
3 Can I leave a message?

Oui, bien sûr.
4 It's fine for the
appointment on
Monday at 11am.

Très bien, au revoir.
5 Thank you, goodbye.

3 Clothing (3 minutes)

Say the French words for the numbered items of clothing.

tie **1**
2 jacket
4 skirt
trousers **3**
6 tights
shoes **5**

3 Clothing

1 la cravate
lah kravat

2 la veste
lah vest

3 le pantalon
luh poñtaloñ

4 la jupe
lah joop

5 les chaussures
lay shohsyur

6 les collants
lay kolloñ

4 At the doctor's (4 minutes)

Say these phrases in French.

1 I don't feel well.
2 Do I need tests?
3 I have a heart condition.
4 Do I need to go to hospital?
5 I am pregnant.

4 At the doctor's

1 Je ne me sens pas bien.
juh nuh muh soñ puh byañ

2 J'ai besoin de tests.
jay buzwañ duh test

3 J'ai un problème au cœur.
jay uñ prob-lem oh kur

4 J'ai besoin d'aller à l'hôpital.
jay buzwañ dallay ah lopeetal

5 Je suis enceinte.
juh swee zoñsant

CHEZ NOUS
At home

1 **Warm up** (1 minute)

Say the months of the year in French. (pp.28-9)

Ask "Is there an art gallery?" (pp.48-9) and "How many brothers do you have?" (pp.14-5)

Many city-dwellers live in an apartment block (**l'immeuble**), but in rural areas the houses tend to be detached (**individuelle**). If you want to know the total number of rooms you will need to ask "**Combien de pièces?**". If you want to know how many bedrooms, ask "**Combien de chambres?**"

2 **Match and repeat** (5 minutes)

Match the numbered items to the list and test yourself using the flap.

❶ la fenêtre
lah fenaytruh

❷ la cheminée
lah shemnay

❸ le toit
lah twut

❹ la gouttière
lah gootyair

❺ le mur
luh myur

❻ le volet
luh volay

❼ la porte
lah port

❽ le passage
luh passarj

chimney ❷

window ❶

❺ wall   ❻ shutter

Cultural tip Most French houses have shutters (**volets**) at each window. These are closed at night and in the heat of the day. Curtains, where they are present, tend to be more for decoration. A single-storey bungalow is known as **un pavillon** and these are popular among the French as holiday homes in tourist resorts.

3 Words to remember (4 minutes)

Quel est le loyer par mois?
kel ay luh lwayay par mwah?
What is the rent per month?

Familiarize yourself with these words and test yourself using the flap.

room	**la pièce** *lah piyes*
floor	**le sol** *luh sol*
ceiling	**le plafond** *luh plafoñ*
bedroom	**la chambre** *lah shombruh*
bathroom	**la salle de bains** *lah sal duh bañ*
kitchen	**la cuisine** *lah kwiseen*
dining room	**la salle à manger** *lah sal ah moñjay*
living room	**le salon** *luh saloñ*
cellar	**la cave** *lah kav*
attic	**le grenier** *luh grunyay*

3 roof

4 gutter

8 driveway   door **7**

4 Useful phrases (3 minutes)

Learn these phrases and test yourself.

Il y a un garage?
eelyah uh gararj

Is there a garage?

C'est disponible quand?
say deesponeebluh koñ

When is it available?

C'est meublé?
say murblay

Is it furnished?

5 Say it (2 minutes)

Is there a dining room?

Is it large?

Is it available in July?

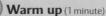

1 Warm up (1 minute)

What is the French for "room" (pp.58-9), "desk" (pp.80-1), "bed" (pp.60-1), and "toilet(s)"? (pp.52-3)

How do you say "soft", "beautiful", and "big"? (pp.64-5)

DANS LA MAISON
In the house

When you rent a house or villa in France, it is usual to be asked to pay for services such as electricity and gas in addition to the basic weekly or monthly rent. Additional charges might also extend to wood or other fuel for an open fire, which is usually charged by the cubic metre.

2 Match and repeat (3 minutes)

Match the numbered items to the list in the panel on the left. Then test yourself by concealing the French with the cover flap.

1 le plan de travail
luh plañ duh traveye

2 l'évier (m)
levyay

3 le micro-ondes
luh meekro-ond

4 la cuisinière
lah kwiseenyair

5 le four
luh foor

6 le frigo
luh freegoh

7 la table
lah tabluh

8 la chaise
lah shez

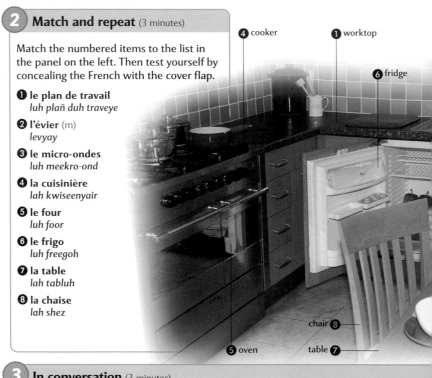

4 cooker   **1** worktop   **6** fridge

chair **8**

5 oven   table **7**

3 In conversation (3 minutes)

C'est le four.
say luh foor

This is the oven.

Il y a un lave-vaisselle aussi?
eelyah uñ lav-vaysel osee

Is there a dishwasher as well?

Oui, et il y a un grand congélateur.
wee, ay eelyah uñ groñ koñjelatur

Yes, and there's a big freezer.

4 Words to remember (2 minutes)

Familiarize yourself with these words and test yourself using the flap.

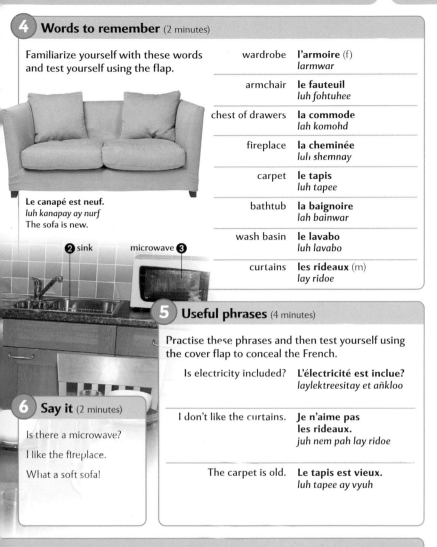

Le canapé est neuf.
luh kanapay ay nurf
The sofa is new.

wardrobe	**l'armoire** (f) *larmwar*	
armchair	**le fauteuil** *luh fohtuhee*	
chest of drawers	**la commode** *lah komohd*	
fireplace	**la cheminée** *luh shemnay*	
carpet	**le tapis** *luh tapee*	
bathtub	**la baignoire** *lah bainwar*	
wash basin	**le lavabo** *luh lavabo*	
curtains	**les rideaux** (m) *lay ridoe*	

❷ sink   microwave ❸

5 Useful phrases (4 minutes)

Practise these phrases and then test yourself using the cover flap to conceal the French.

Is electricity included?	**L'électricité est inclue?** *laylektreesitay et añkloo*
I don't like the curtains.	**Je n'aime pas les rideaux.** *juh nem pah lay ridoe*
The carpet is old.	**Le tapis est vieux.** *luh tapee ay vyuh*

6 Say it (2 minutes)

Is there a microwave?

I like the fireplace.

What a soft sofa!

L'évier est neuf?
levyay ay nurf

Is the sink new?

Bien sûr. Et voilà la machine à laver.
byañ syur. ay vwalah lah masheen ah lavay

Of course. And here's the washing machine.

Quel beau carrelage!
kel boe karlarj

What beautiful tiles!

LE JARDIN
The garden

1 **Warm up** (1 minute)

Say "I need", "you need", "he needs". (pp.64-5, pp.92-4)

What is the French for "day", "week", and "month"? (pp.28-9)

Say the days of the week. (pp.28-9)

The garden of a house or villa may be communal, or at least partly shared. Check with the estate agent. In general, French gardens are well-kept and reasonably formal. The natural, "wild" look is not very popular and hedges are usually carefully trimmed and lawns are regularly mown.

2 **Words to remember** (3 minutes)

Familiarize yourself with these words and test yourself using the flap.

la tondeuse à gazon *lah toñdurz ah gazoñ*	lawn mower
la fourche *lah foorsh*	fork
la bêche *lah besh*	spade
le râteau *luh ratoe*	rake
la jardinerie *lah jardañree*	garden centre

terrace ❶

tree ❷

flowers ❼

❽ weeds

soil ❸

path ❾

3 Useful phrases (4 minutes)

Familarize yourself with these phrases and then test yourself.

The gardener comes once a week.	**Le jardinier vient une fois par semaine.** *luh jardañyay vyañ oon fwah par suhmayn*
Can you mow the lawn?	**Vous pouvez tondre la pelouse?** *voo poovay toñdruh lah pelooz*
Is the garden private?	**Le jardin est privé?** *luh jardañ ay preevay*
The garden needs watering.	**Le jardin a besoin d'eau.** *luh jardañ ah buzwañ doe*

4 Match and repeat (5 minutes)

Match the numbered items to the words in the panel on the right.

5 hedge
4 lawn
6 plants
10 flowerbed

1 **la terrasse**
lah terass

2 **l'arbre** (m)
larbruh

3 **la terre**
lah tair

4 **la pelouse**
lah pelooz

5 **la haie**
lah ay

6 **les plantes** (f)
lay ploñt

7 **les fleurs** (f)
lay flur

8 **les mauvaises herbes** (f)
lay movay zurb

9 **l'allée** (f)
lallay

10 **le parterre de fleurs**
luh partair duh flur

5 Say it (2 minutes)

The lawn needs watering.

Are there any trees?

The gardener comes on Fridays.

LES ANIMAUX
Pets

1 **Warm up** (1 minute)

Say "My name's John".
(pp.8-9)

How do you say "Don't
worry"? (pp.94-5)

What's "your" in French?
(pp.12-3)

"Pet passports" are now available to enable
holiday-makers and commuters to take their
pets with them to France and avoid quarantine
on return to the United Kingdom. Consult your
vet for details of how to obtain the necessary
vaccinations and paperwork.

2 **Match and repeat** (3 minutes)

Match the numbered animals to the French
words in the panel on the left. Then test
yourself using the cover flap.

❶ le chat
 luh shah

❷ le lapin
 luh lapañ

❸ l'oiseau (m)
 lwazoe

❹ le poisson
 luh pwassoñ

❺ le chien
 luh shiañ

❻ le hamster
 luh amstair

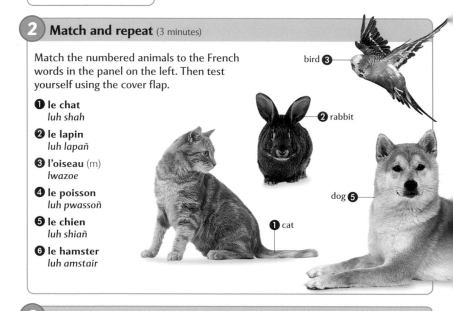

bird ❸

❷ rabbit

dog ❺

❶ cat

3 **Useful phrases** (4 minutes)

Familiarize yourself with these phrases and
then test yourself using the cover flap.

Ce chien est gentil? *suh shiañ ay joñtee*	Is this dog friendly?
Je peux amener mon chien? *juh puh amunay moñ shiañ*	Can I bring my dog?
J'ai peur des chats. *jay pur day shah*	I'm frightened of cats.
Mon chien ne mord pas. *moñ shiañ nuh mor pah*	My dog doesn't bite.

Ce chat est plein de puces.
suh shah ay plañ duh pous
This cat is full of fleas.

Cultural tip Many dogs in France are guard dogs and you may encounter them tethered or roaming free. Approach farms and rural houses with care, and keep away from the dog's territory. Look out for warning notices such as **Attention au chien** (*Beware of the dog*).

ATTENTION AU CHIEN

Mon chien est malade.
moñ shiañ ay malahd
My dog is not well.

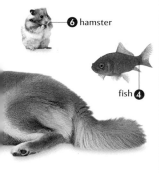

❻ hamster

fish ❹

4 **Words to remember** (4 minutes)

Memorize these words and test yourself using the cover flap.

vet	**le vétérinaire** *luh vetairinair*
vaccination	**la vaccination** *lah vaksinasyoñ*
pet passport	**le passeport d'animaux** *luh passpor danimoe*
basket	**le panier** *luh panyay*
cage	**la cage** *lah karj*
bowl	**la gamelle** *lah gamel*
collar	**le collier** *luh kolyay*
lead	**la laisse** *lah less*
fleas	**les puces** (f) *lay pous*

5 **Put into practice** (3 minutes)

Join in this conversation. Read the French on the left and follow the instructions to make your reply. Then test yourself by concealing the answers with the cover flap.

C'est votre chien?
say votruh shiañ

Is this your dog?

Say: Yes, he's called Sandy.

Oui, il s'appelle Sandy.
wee, eel sapell Sandy

J'ai peur des chiens.
jay pur day shiañ

I'm frightened of dogs.

Say: Don't worry. He's friendly.

Ne vous inquiétez pas. Il est gentil.
nuh voo zañkyatay pah. eel ay joñtee

Réponses
Answers (Cover with flap)

RÉVISEZ ET RÉPÉTEZ
Review and repeat

1 **Colours**

1 **Colours** (4 minutes)

Complete the sentences with the French for the colour in brackets. Be careful to choose the correct masculine or feminine form.

❶ Vous avez cette veste en _____ ? (black)

❷ Je prends la jupe _____. (white)

❸ Vous avez cette robe en _____? (red)

❹ Non mais j'ai une _____. (green)

❺ Vous avez des chaussettes _____?
(yellow)

❶ **noir**
nwar

❷ **blanche**
blonsh

❸ **rouge**
rooj

❹ **verte**
vairt

❺ **jaunes**
jon

2 **Kitchen**

❶ **la cuisinière**
lah kwiseenyair

❷ **le frigo**
luh freegoh

❸ **l'évier**
levyay

❹ **le micro-ondes**
luh meekro-ond

❺ **le four**
luh foor

❻ **la chaise**
lah shez

❼ **la table**
lah tabluh

2 **Kitchen** (4 minutes)

Say the French words for the numbered items.

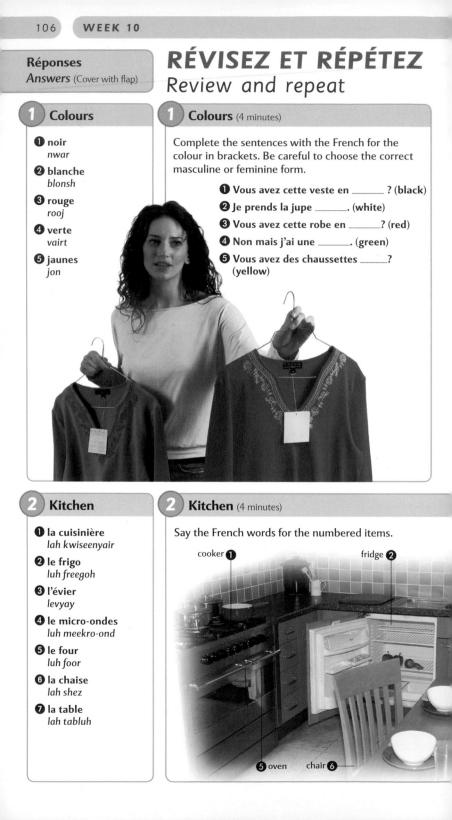

cooker ❶   fridge ❷

❺ oven   chair ❻

Réponses
Answers (Cover with flap)

3 House (4 minutes)

You are visiting a house in France. Join in the conversation, replying in French following the English prompts.

Voilà le salon.
① What a lovely fireplace!

Oui, et il y a aussi une grande cuisine.
② How many bedrooms?

Il y a trois chambres.
③ Do you have a garage?

Non, mais il y a un grand jardin.
④ When is it available?

Juillet.
⑤ What is the rent a month?

3 House

① Quelle belle cheminée!
kel bel shemnay

② Combien de chambres?
koñbyañ duh shombruh

③ Vous avez un garage?
voo zavay uñ gararj

④ C'est disponible quand?
say deesponeebluh koñ

⑤ Quel est le loyer par mois?
kel ay luh lwayay par mwah

4 At home (3 minutes)

Say the French for the following items:

① washing machine
② sofa
③ attic
④ dining room
⑤ tree
⑥ garden

microwave ④

③ sink

table ⑦

4 At home

① la machine à laver
lah masheen ah lavay

② le canapé
luh kanapay

③ le grenier
luh grunyay

④ la salle à manger
lah sal ah moñjay

⑤ l'arbre
larbruh

⑥ le jardin
luh jardañ

1 **Warm up** (1 minute)

Ask "How do I get to the bank?" and "How do I get to the post office?" (pp.68-9)

What's the French for "passport"? (pp.54-5)

Ask "What time?" (pp.30-1)

LA POSTE ET LA BANQUE
Post and bank

The post office also serves as a bank. You do not need to queue at the cashier, as there are normally cashpoints available outside the building. Stamps are also available from **le tabac** (bar/tobacconists).

2 **Words to remember: post** (3 minutes)

la boîte postale *lah bwat post-tal*	post box
la carte postale *lah kart post-tal*	postcard
le colis *luh kolee*	parcel
par avion *par avyoñ*	air mail
en recommandé *oñ rukomoñday*	registered post
le timbre *luh tambruh*	stamp
le code postal *luh kod post-tal*	postcode
le facteur *luh faktur*	postman

Familiarize yourself with these words and test yourself using the cover flap to conceal the French on the left.

C'est combien pour le Royaume-Uni?
say koñbyañ poor luh royom oonee
How much is it for the United Kingdom?

l'enveloppe (f)
loñvuhlop
envelope

3 **In conversation** (3 minutes)

Je voudrais retirer de l'argent.
juh voodray ruteeray duh larjoñ

I'd like to withdraw some money.

Vous avez une identification?
voo zavay oon eedoñtee-fikasyoñ

Do you have any identification?

Oui, voilà mon passeport.
wee, vwalah moñ passpor

Yes, here's my passport.

la carte bancaire
lah kart boñkair
bank card

Comment je peux payer?
komon juh puh payay
How can I pay?

4 Words to remember: bank (2 minutes)

Familiarize yourself with these words and test yourself using the cover flap to conceal the French on the right.

PIN	**le code** *luh kod*
bank	**la banque** *lah boñk*
cashier	**le guichet** *luh geeshay*
notes	**les billets** *lay beeyay*
ATM/cashpoint	**le distributeur automatique** *luh distreebootur otomateek*
travellers' cheques	**les chèques de voyage** *lay shek duh vwoyarj*

5 Useful phrases (4 minutes)

Learn these phrases and then test yourself using the cover flap.

I'd like to change some money.	**Je voudrais changer de l'argent.** *juh voodray shoñjay duh larjoñ*
What is the exchange rate?	**Quel est le taux de change?** *kel ay luh toe duh shoñj*
I'd like to withdraw some money.	**Je voudrais retirer de l'argent.** *juh voodray ruteeray duh larjoñ*

6 Say it (2 minutes)

I'd like a stamp for the United Kingdom.

I'd like to change some travellers' cheques.

Do I need my passport?

Composez votre code s'il vous plaît.
komposay votruh kod seel voo play

Please key in your PIN.

J'ai besoin de signer aussi?
jay buzwañ duh seenyay ohsee

Do I need to sign as well?

Non, ce n'est pas nécessaire.
noñ, suh nay pah nesesair

No, that's not necessary.

LES SERVICES
Services

1 **Warm up** (1 minute)

What's the French for "doesn't work"? (pp.60-1)

Say "today" and "tomorrow". (pp.28-9)

You can combine the French words on these pages with the vocabulary you learned in week 10 to help you explain basic problems and cope with arranging most repairs. When organizing building work or a repair, it's a good idea to agree the price and method of payment in advance.

2 **Words to remember** (4 minutes)

Familiarize yourself with these words and test yourself using the flap.

le plombier *luh ploñbyay*	plumber
l'électricien (m) *laylektreesyañ*	electrician
le garagiste *luh gararjeest*	mechanic
le constructeur *luh koñstruktur*	builder
la femme de ménage *lah fam duh maynarj*	cleaner
le décorateur *luh daykoratur*	decorator
le charpentier *luh sharpañtyay*	carpenter
le maçon *luh massoñ*	bricklayer

la manivelle
lah maneevel
wrench

Je n'ai pas besoin d'un garagiste.
juh nay pah buzwañ duñ gararjeest
I don't need a mechanic.

3 **In conversation** (3 minutes)

La machine à laver est en panne.
lah masheen ah lavay ay toñ pan

The washing machine has broken down.

Oui, le tuyeau est cassé.
wee luh tweeyoh ay kassay

Yes, the hose is broken.

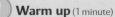

Vous pouvez la réparer?
voo poovay lah rayparay

Can you repair it?

SERVICES 111

4 Useful phrases (3 minutes)

Learn these phrases and then test yourself using the cover flap.

Je peux faire réparer ça où?
juh puh fair rayparay sah oo
Where can I get this repaired?

Please clean the bathroom.	**Nettoyez la salle de bain, s'il vous plait.** *netwuhyay lah sal duh bañ seel voo play*
Can you repair the boiler?	**Vous pouvez réparer la chaudière?** *voo poovay rayparay lah shodyair*
Do you know a good electrician?	**Vous connaissez un bon électricien?** *voo konessay uñ boñ aylektreesyañ*

5 Put into practice (4 minutes)

Practise these phrases. Cover up the text on the right and complete the dialogue in French. Check your answers and repeat if necessary.

Votre clôture est cassée.
votruh klotoor ay kassay

Your fence is broken.

Ask: Do you know a good builder?

Vous connaissez un bon constructeur?
voo konessay uh boñ koñstruktur

Oui, il y en a un dans le village.
wee, eelyonah uñ doñ luh villarj

Yes, there is one in the village.

Ask: Do you have his phone number?

Vous avez son numéro de téléphone?
voo zavay soñ noomairoe duh telayfon

Non, vous avez besoin d'un nouveau.
noñ. voo zavay buzwañ duñ noovoh

No, you need a new one.

Vous pouvez faire ça aujourd'hui?
voo poovay fair sah oh-joordwee

Can you do it today?

Non, je reviens demain.
non, juh ruvyañ dumañ

No. I'll come back tomorrow.

1 Warm up (1 minute)

Say the days of the week in French. (pp.28-9)

How do you say "cleaner"? (pp.110-11)

Say "It's 9.30", "10.45", and "12.00". (pp.10-11, pp.30-1)

VENIR
To come

The verb **venir** (*to come*) is another important verb. Other useful verbs are made up of **venir** with a prefix, such as **revenir** (*to come back*) and **devenir** (*to become*). These can be formed in the same way as **venir** (below). Remember that **je viens** can mean either *I come* or *I am coming*.

2 Venir: to come (6 minutes)

Say the different forms of **venir** (*to come*) aloud. Use the cover flap to test yourself and, when you are confident, practise the sample sentences below.

je viens *juh vyañ*	I come
tu viens *tew vyañ*	you come (informal singular)
il/elle vient *eel/el vyañ*	he/she comes
nous venons *noo vunoñ*	we come
vous venez *voo vunay*	you come (formal singular or plural)
ils/elles viennent *eel/el vyen*	they come
Je viens de New York. *juh vyañ duh noo york*	I come from New York.
Nous venons tous les mardis. *noo vunoñ too lay mardee*	We come every Tuesday.
Ils viennent par le train. *eel vyen par luh trañ*	They come by train.

Il vient de Chine.
eel vyañ duh sheen
He comes from China.

Conversational tip You can use the phrase **je viens de...** (literally *I come from...*) to talk about something you have just done or have recently completed. For example **je viens de faire les courses** (*I have just done the shopping*) or **je viens d'envoyer un email** (*I have just sent an e-mail*). To say *just* in the sense of *only*, as in *I eat just a sandwich for lunch*, the French use **seulement**: **je mange seulement un sandwich pour déjeuner**.

3 Useful phrases (4 minutes)

Learn these phrases and then test yourself using the cover flap.

When can I come?	**Je peux venir quand?** *juh puh vuneer koñ*
Where does she come from?	**Elle vient d'où?** *el vyañ doo*
The cleaner comes every Monday.	**La femme de ménage vient tous les lundis.** *lah fam duh maynarj vyañ too lay luñdee*
Come with me. (informal/formal)	**Viens avec moi./ Venez avec moi.** *vyañ avek mwah/ vunay avek mwah*

Je viens de me réveiller.
juh vyañ duh muh rayvay-yay
I have just woken up.

4 Put into practice (4 minutes)

Join in this conversation. Read the French on the left and follow the instructions to make your reply. Then test yourself by concealing the answers with the cover flap.

Bonjour, salon de coiffure Christine.
boñjoor, saloñ duh kwafur Christine

Hello, this is Christine's hair salon.

Say: I'd like an appointment.

Je voudrais un rendez-vous.
juh voodray uñ roñday-voo

Vous voulez venir quand?
voo voolay vuneer koñ

When do you want to come?

Say: Can I come today?

Je peux venir aujourd'hui?
juh puh vuneer oh-joordwee

Oui bien sûr, à quelle heure?
wee byañ syur, ah kel ur

Yes of course, what time?

Say: At 10.30.

A dix heures et demie.
ah deez ur ay dumee

1 Warm up (1 minute)

What's the French for "big/tall" and "small/short"? (pp.64-5)

Say "The room is big" and "The bed is small". (pp.64-5)

LA POLICE ET LE CRIME
Police and crime

If you are the victim of a crime while in France, you should go to a police station to report it. In an emergency you can dial 112. You may have to explain your complaint in French, so some basic vocabulary is useful. In the event of a burglary, the police will usually come to the house.

2 Words to remember: crime (4 minutes)

Familiarize yourself with these words.

le cambriolage *luh kañbryolarj*	burglary
le rapport de police *luh rapor duh polees*	police report
le voleur *luh volur*	thief
la police *lah polees*	police
la déposition *lah daypoziyoñ*	statement
le témoin *luh taymwañ*	witness
l'avocat(e) *lavokah(aht)*	lawyer

J'ai besoin d'un avocat.
jay buzwañ duñ avokah
I need a lawyer.

3 Useful phrases (3 minutes)

Memorize these phrases and then test yourself using the cover flap.

J'ai été cambriolé(e). *jay aytay kañbryolay*	I've been burgled.
Qu'est-ce qui a été volé? *keskee ah aytay volay*	What was stolen?
Vous avez vu qui a fait ça? *voo zavay voo kee ah fay sah*	Did you see who did it?
Ça s'est passé quand? *sah say passay koñ*	When did it happen?

l'appareil-photo
lapareye foto
camera

le porte-monnaie
luh port mohnay
purse

4 Words to remember: appearance (5 minutes)

Learn these words. Remember some adjectives have a feminine form.

Il est chauve avec une barbe.
eel ay shohv avek oon barb
He is bald and has a beard.

Il a les cheveux noirs et courts.
eel ah lay shuvuh nwar ay kor
He has short, black hair.

man	**l'homme** (m)	*lom*
woman	**la femme**	*lah fam*
tall	**grand/grande**	*groñ/groñd*
short	**petit/petite**	*puhtee/puhteet*
young	**jeune**	*juhn*
old	**vieux/vieille**	*vyuh/vyay*
fat	**gros/grosse**	*groe/gros*
thin	**maigre**	*maygruh*
long/short hair	**les cheveux longs/courts** (m)	*lay shuvuh loñ/kor*
spectacles	**les lunettes** (f)	*lay loonet*
beard	**la barbe**	*lah barb*

Cultural tip In France there is a difference between **la gendarmerie** and **la police**. **La gendarmerie** operates in smaller towns and **la police** in major cities. Their appearance and uniform are similar and officers from both forces carry guns.

5 Put into practice (2 minutes)

Practise these phrases. Then cover up the text on the right and follow the instructions to make your reply in French.

Il ressemblait à quoi?
eel ruzoñblay ah kwah

What did he look like?

Say: Short and fat.

Petit et gros.
puhtee ay groe

Et les cheveux?
ay lay shuvuh

And the hair?

Say: Long with a beard.

Longs avec une barbe.
loñ avek oon barb

RÉVISEZ ET RÉPÉTEZ
Review and repeat

1 To come

1 viviens
vyañ

2 vient
vyañ

3 venons
vunoñ

4 venez
vunay

5 viennent
vyen

1 To come (3 minutes)

Put the correct form of **venir** (*to come*) into the gaps.

1 Je _____ à quatre heures.

2 Le jardinier _____ une fois par semaine.

3 Nous _____ pour déjeuner mardi.

4 Vous _____ avec nous?

5 Mes parents _____ par le train.

2 Bank and post

1 les billets
lay biyay

2 les timbres
lay tambruh

3 la carte bancaire
lah kart boñkair

4 les cartes postales
lay kart post-tal

5 le colis
luh kolee

2 Bank and post (4 minutes)

Say the French words for the following numbered items:

stamps **2**

1 notes

postcard **4**

bank card **3**

parcel **5**

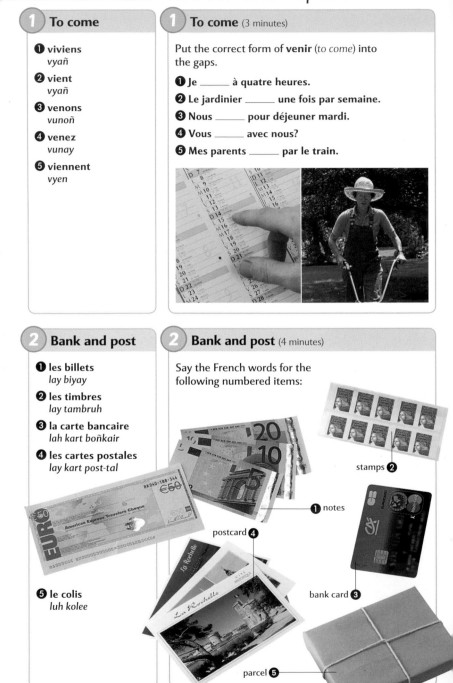

3 Appearance (4 minutes)

What do these descriptions mean?

❶ C'est un homme grand et maigre.

❷ Elle a les cheveux courts et des lunettes.

❸ Je suis petite et j'ai les cheveux longs.

❹ Elle est vieille et grosse.

❺ Il a les yeux bleus et une barbe.

3 Appearance

❶ He's a tall thin man.
❷ She has short hair and glasses.
❸ I'm short and I have long hair.
❹ She is old and fat.
❺ He has blue eyes and a beard.

4 The pharmacy (4 minutes)

You are asking a pharmacist for advice. Join in the conversation, replying in French following the English prompts.

Bonjour. Je peux vous aider?
❶ I have a cough.

Et vous avez aussi un rhume?
❷ No, but I have a headache.

Prenez ces cachets.
❸ Do you have that as a syrup?

Bien sûr. Voilà.
❹ Thank you. How much is that?

Six euros.
❺ Here you are. Goodbye.

4 The pharmacy

❶ J'ai une toux.
jay oon too

❷ Non, mai j'ai mal à la tête.
noñ. may jay mal ah lah tet

❸ Vous avez un sirop à la place?
voo zavay uñ seeroe ah lah plas

❹ Merci. C'est combien?
mairsee. say koñbyañ

❺ Voilà. Au revoir.
vwalah. ovwar

LES LOISIRS
Leisure time

The French pride themselves on their support for the arts, including opera and film. It would not be unusual to number politics or philosophy among your interests. Phrasebooks aimed at French speakers often have a section on useful conversational openers for these topics.

1 Warm up (1 minute)

What is the French for "museum" and "art gallery"? (pp.48-9)

Say "I don't like the curtains". (pp.100-1)

Ask "Do you want...?" informally (pp.22-3)

2 Words to remember (4 minutes)

Familiarize yourself with these words and test yourself using the cover flap to conceal the French on the left.

le théâtre *luh tay-atruh*	theatre
le cinéma *luh sinaymah*	cinema
la discothèque *lah diskotek*	disco
la musique *lah moozeek*	music
l'art (m) *lar*	art
le sport *luh spor*	sport
le tourisme *luh torizmuh*	sightseeing
les jeux vidéos *lay juh viday-oh*	computer games

J'adore l'opéra.
jador lopayra
I love opera.

3 In conversation (4 minutes)

Salut, tu veux jouer au tennis aujourd'hui?
saloo, tew vuh jooay oh tenees oh-joordwee

Hi, do you want to play tennis today?

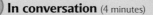

Non. Je n'aime pas le sport.
noñ. juh nem pah luh spor

No, I don't like sport.

Alors, quels sont tes intérêts?
alor, kel soñ tay zañtairay

So what are your interests?

Je déteste la guitare.
juh daytest lah geetar
I hate guitar music.

les spectateurs (m)
lay spektahtur
audience

la galerie
lah galuree
circle

l'orchestre (m)
lorkestruh
stalls

4 Useful phrases (4 minutes)

Learn these phrases and then test yourself using the cover flap.

What are your (formal/informal) interests?	**Quels sont vos/tes intérêts?** *kel soñ voe/tay zañtayray*
I like the theatre.	**J'aime le théâtre.** *jem luh tay-atruh*
I prefer the cinema.	**Je préfère le cinéma.** *juh prayfair luh sinaymah*
I'm interested in art.	**Je m'intéresse à l'art.** *juh mañtairess ah lar*
That bores me.	**Ça m'ennuie.** *sah moñwee*

5 Say it (2 minutes)

I'm interested in music.

I prefer sport.

I don't like computer games.

Je préfère le shopping.
juh prayfair luh shopping

I prefer shopping.

Ça ne m'intéresse pas.
sah nuh mañtairess pah

That doesn't interest me.

Pas de problème. J'y vais toute seule.
pah de prob-lem. jee vay toot surl

No problem. I'll go on my own.

LE SPORT ET LES PASSE-TEMPS
Sport and hobbies

1 Warm up (1 minute)

Ask "Do you (formal) want to play tennis?" (pp.118-19)

Say "I like the theatre" and "I prefer sightseeing". (pp.118-19)

Say "That doesn't interest me". (pp.118-19)

The verb **faire** (to do or to make) is a useful verb for talking about hobbies. **Faire** is followed by **du, de la** or **de l': Je fais de la peinture** (I paint). You can also use the verb **jouer** (to play) when talking about playing sports and music.

2 Words to remember (5 minutes)

Memorize these words and then test yourself.

le football/rugby *luh futbohl/roogbee*	football/rugby
le tennis *luh tenees*	tennis
la natation *lah natasyoñ*	swimming
la voile *lah vwal*	sailing
la pêche *lah pesh*	fishing
la peinture *lah pañtyur*	painting
le vélo *luh vaylo*	cycling
la randonnée *lah rañdonay*	hiking

le bunker
luh bañkuh
bunker

le joueur
de golf
*luh joowur
duh golf*
golfer

Je joue au golf tout les jours.
*juh joo oh golf
too lay joor*
I play golf
every day.

3 Useful phrases (2 minutes)

Familiarize yourself with these phrases.

Je fais du rugby. *juh fay doo roogbee*	I play rugby.
Il joue au tennis. *eel joo oh tenees*	He plays tennis.
Elle fait de la peinture. *el fay duh lah pañtyur*	She paints.

4 Faire: to do or to make (4 minutes)

Il fait beau aujourd'hui.
eel fay boe oh-joordwee
It's nice weather today.

___ **le drapeau**
luh drapoh
flag

___ **le parcours de golf**
luh parkoor duh golf
golf course

The verb **faire** (*to do or to make*) is also used to describe the weather. Learn its different forms and practise the sample sentences below.

I do	**je fais** *juh fay*
you do (informal)	**tu fais** *tew fay*
he/she does	**il/elle fait** *eel/el fay*
we do	**nous faisons** *noo fayzon*
you do (formal/plural)	**vous faites** *voo fet*
they do	**ils/elles font** *eel/el foñ*
I go hiking.	**Je fais de la randonnée.** *juh fay duh lah rañdonay*
What do you do?	**Que faites-vous?** *kuh fet voo*
We play tennis.	**Nous faisons du tennis.** *noo fayzon doo tenees*

5 Put into practice (3 minutes)

Practise these phrases. Then cover the text on the right and complete the dialogue in French. Check your answers.

Qu'est-ce que vous aimez faire?
keskuh voo zemay fair

What do you like doing?

Say: I like playing tennis.

J'aime jouer au tennis.
jem jooway oh tenees

Tu fais du football aussi?
tew fay doo futbohl ohsee

Do you play football as well?

Say: No. I play rugby.

Non, je fais du rugby.
noñ, juh fay doo roogbee

Cultural tip France boasts a huge variety of regional games, such as pelota in the Basque country. Most popular of all, the French version of bowls - **pétanque** or **boules** - is played in almost every town and village.

1 Warm up (1 minute)

Say "my husband" and "my wife". (pp.10-11)

How do you say "lunch" and "dinner" in French? (pp.20-1)

Say "Sorry, I'm busy". (pp.32-3)

VOIR DES GENS
Socializing

The French dinner table is the centre of their social world. You can expect to do a lot of your socializing enjoying food and wine. It is best to use the more polite **vous** form to talk to people you meet socially until they call you **tu**, in which case you can reciprocate.

2 Useful phrases (3 minutes)

Learn these phrases and then test yourself.

l'invitée (f)
lanveetay
guest

Je voudrais vous inviter à dîner. *juh voodray voo zañveetay ah deenay*	I'd like to invite you for dinner.
Vous êtes libre mercredi prochain? *voo zet leebruh mairkrudee prochen*	Are you free next Wednesday?
Une autre fois peut-être. *oon awtruh fwah putetruh*	Another time perhaps.

Cultural tip When you go to someone's house for the first time, it is usual to bring flowers or wine. If you are invited again, having seen your host's house, you can bring something a little more personal.

3 In conversation (3 minutes)

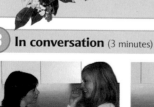

Vous voulez venir dîner mardi?
voo voolay vuneer deenay mardee

Would you like to come to dinner on Tuesday?

Je suis désolée, je suis occupée.
juh swee dayzolay, juh swee zokoopay

I'm sorry, I'm busy.

Pourquoi pas jeudi?
poorkwah pah jurdee

What about Thursday?

4 Words to remember (3 minutes)

Familiarize yourself with these words and test yourself using the flap.

l'hôtesse (f)
lohtess
hostess

party	**la soirée** *lah swaray*
dinner party	**le dîner** *luh deenay*
invitation	**l'invitation** *lañveetasyoñ*
reception	**la réception** *lah raysepsyoñ*
cocktail party	**le cocktail** *luh koktail*

5 Put into practice (5 minutes)

Join in this conversation.

Vous pouvez venir à une réception ce soir.
voo poovay vuneer ah oon raysepsyoñ suh swah

Can you come to a reception this evening?

Say: Yes, I'd love to.

Oui, avec plaisir.
wee, avek playzeer

Merci de nous avoir invités.
mairsee duh noo zavwar añveetay
Thank you for inviting us.

Ça commence à huit heures.
sah komoñs ah weet ur

It starts at eight o'clock.

Ask: Should I dress formally?

Il faut s'habiller?
eel foe sabeeyay

Avec plaisir.
avek playzeer

With pleasure.

Venez avec votre mari.
vunay avek votruh maree

Please bring your husband.

Merci. A quelle heure?
mairsee. ah kel ur

Thank you. At what time?

Réponses
Answers (Cover with flap)

RÉVISEZ ET RÉPÉTEZ
Review and repeat

1 Animals

❶ **le poisson**
luh pwassoñ

❷ **l'oiseau**
lwazoe

❸ **le lapin**
luh lapañ

❹ **le chat**
luh shah

❺ **le hamster**
luh amstair

❻ **le chien**
luh shiañ

1 Animals (3 minutes)

Say the French words for the numbered animals.

rabbit ❸

❶ fish

hamster ❺

❹ cat

2 I like...

❶ **J'aime le rugby.**
jem luh roogbee

❷ **Je n'aime pas le golf.**
juh nem pah luh golf

❸ **J'aime faire de la peinture.**
jem fair duh lah pañtyur

❹ **Je n'aime pas jouer aux boules.**
juh nem pah jooway oh bool

2 I like... (4 minutes)

Say the following in French.

❶ I like rugby.
❷ I don't like golf.
❸ I like painting.
❹ I don't like playing boules.

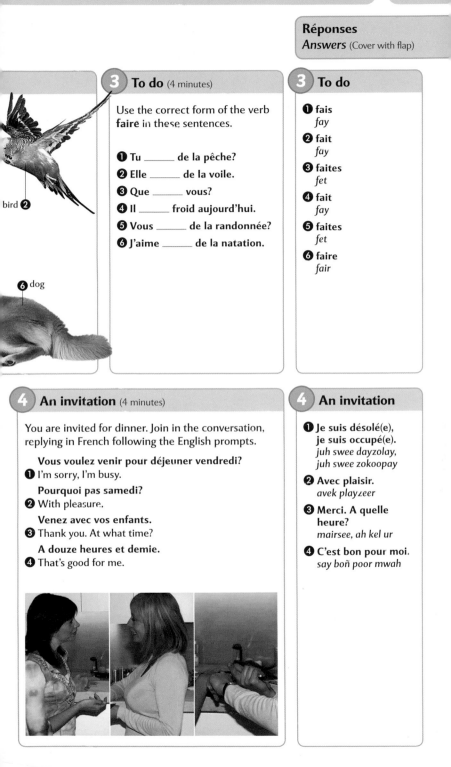

bird ②

⑥ dog

3 To do (4 minutes)

Use the correct form of the verb **faire** in these sentences.

① Tu _____ de la pêche?
② Elle _____ de la voile.
③ Que _____ vous?
④ Il _____ froid aujourd'hui.
⑤ Vous _____ de la randonnée?
⑥ J'aime _____ de la natation.

3 To do

① **fais**
fay
② **fait**
fay
③ **faites**
fet
④ **fait**
fay
⑤ **faites**
fet
⑥ **faire**
fair

4 An invitation (4 minutes)

You are invited for dinner. Join in the conversation, replying in French following the English prompts.

Vous voulez venir pour déjeuner vendredi?
① I'm sorry, I'm busy.

Pourquoi pas samedi?
② With pleasure.

Venez avec vos enfants.
③ Thank you. At what time?

A douze heures et demie.
④ That's good for me.

4 An invitation

① **Je suis désolé(e), je suis occupé(e).**
juh swee dayzolay, juh swee zokoopay

② **Avec plaisir.**
avek playzeer

③ **Merci. A quelle heure?**
mairsee, ah kel ur

④ **C'est bon pour moi.**
say boñ poor mwah

Reinforce and progress

Regular practice is the key to maintaining and advancing your language skills. In this section you will find a variety of suggestions for reinforcing and extending your knowledge of French. Many involve returning to exercises in the book and using the dictionaries to extend their scope. Go back through the lessons in a different order, mix and match activities to make up your own 15-minute daily programme, or focus on topics that are of particular relevance to your current needs.

1 Warm up (1 minute)

Say "he is" and "they are". (pp.14–15)

Say "he is not" and "they are not". (pp.14–15)

What is French for "the children"? (pp.10–11)

3 I'd like... (3 minutes)

Say you'd like the following:

1 black coffee
jam **2**
bread **3**
large coffee **4** with milk

Keep warmed up
Re-visit the Warm Up boxes to remind yourself of key words and phrases. Make sure you work your way through all of them on a regular basis.

Review and repeat again
Work through a Review and Repeat lesson as a way of reinforcing words and phrases presented in the course. Return to the main lesson for any topic on which you are no longer confident.

3 In conversation: taxi (2 minutes)

Carry on conversing
Re-read the In Conversation panels. Say both parts of the conversation, paying attention to the pronunciation. Where possible, try incorporating new words from the dictionary.

Le marché aux fromages, s'il vous plaît.
luh marshayoe fromarj, seel voo play

The cheese market, please.

Oui, sans problème, monsieur.
wee. soñ problem musyuh

Yes, no problem, sir.

Vous pouvez me dépos⸺ ici, s'il vous plaît?
voo poovay muh dayposa⸺ eesee, seel voo play

Can you drop me ⸺

3 Useful phrases (5 minutes)

Familiarize yourself with these phrases and then test yourself.

The room is too cold/hot.	**La chambre est trop froide/chaude.** *lah shombruh ay troe fwrard/shohd*
There are no towels.	**Il n'y a pas de serviettes.** *eenyah pah duh survyet*
I need some soap.	**J'ai besoin de savon.** *jay buzwañ duh savoñ*
The shower doesn't work very well.	**La douche ne marche pas très bien.** *lah doosh nuh marsh pah tray byañ*

Practise phrases
Return to the Useful Phrases and Put into Practice exercises. Test yourself using the cover flap. When you are confident, devise your own versions of the phrases, using new words from the dictionary.

Match, repeat, and extend
Remind yourself of words related to specific topics by returning to the Match and Repeat and Words to Remember exercises. Test yourself using the cover flap. Discover new words in that area by referring to the dictionary and menu guide.

② lettuce

③ lemons

④ leeks

courgettes ①

② Match and repeat (4 minutes)

Match the numbered items in this scene with the text in the panel.

① les courgettes (f)
lay korjet

② la salade
lah sah-lad

③ les citrons (m)
lay sitroñ

④ les poireaux (m)
lay pwaroe

⑤ les tomates (f)
lay toemat

⑥ les champignons (m)
lay shoñpeeyoñ

⑦ les avocats (m)
lay zavokah

⑧ les pommes de terre (f)
lay pom duh tair

tomatoes **⑤**   **⑥** mushrooms   **⑧** potatoes

avocados **⑦**

Say it again
The Say It exercises are a useful instant reminder for each lesson. Practise these, using your own vocabulary variations from the dictionary or elsewhere in the lesson.

⑤ Say it (2 minutes)

Three kilos of potatoes, please.

The mushrooms are too expensive.

How much is the lettuce?

Using other resources

As well as working with this book, try the following language extension ideas:

Visit a French-speaking country and try out your new skills with native speakers. Find out if there is a French community near you. There may be shops, cafés, restaurants, and clubs. Try to visit some of these and use your French to order food and drink and strike up conversations. Most native speakers will be happy to speak French to you.

Join a language class or club. There are usually evening and day classes available at a variety of different levels. Or you could start a club yourself if you have friends who are also interested in keeping up their French.

Look at French magazines and newspapers. The pictures will help you to understand the text. Advertisements are also a useful way of expanding your vocabulary.

Use the Internet, where you can find all kinds of websites for learning languages, some of which offer free online help and activities. You can also find French websites for everything from renting a house to shampooing your pet. You can even access French radio and TV stations online. Start by going to a French search engine, such as *voila.fr*, and key a subject that interests you, or set yourself a challenge, for example, finding a two-bedroom house for rent by the sea in Normandy.

MENU GUIDE

This guide lists the most common terms you may encounter on French menus or when shopping for food. If you can't find an exact phrase, try looking up its component parts.

A

abats *offal*
abricot *apricot*
à emporter *to take away*
agneau *lamb*
aiguillette de bœuf *slices of rump steak*
ail *garlic*
ailloli *garlic mayonnaise*
à la broche *spit roast*
à la jardinière *with assorted vegetables*
à la normande *in cream sauce*
à la vapeur *steamed*
amande *almond*
ananas *pineapple*
anchois *anchovies*
andouillette *spicy sausage*
anguille *eel*
à point *medium*
artichaut *artichoke*
asperge *asparagus*
assiette anglaise *selection of cold meats*
au gratin *baked in a milk, cream, and cheese sauce*
au vin blanc *in white wine*
avocat *avocado*

B

banane *banana*
barbue *brill (fish)*
bavaroise *light mousse*
béarnaise *with béarnaise sauce*
bécasse *woodcock*
béchamel *white sauce*
beignet *fritter, doughnut*
beignet aux pommes *apple fritter*
betterave *beetroot*
beurre *butter*
beurre d'anchois *anchovy paste*
beurre noir *dark, melted butter*
bien cuit *well done*
bière *beer*
bière à la pression *draught beer*
bière blonde *lager*
bière brune *bitter beer*
bière panachée *shandy*

bifteck *steak*
bisque d'écrevisses *crayfish soup*
bisque de homard *lobster soup*
biscuit de Savoie *sponge cake*
blanquette de veau *veal stew*
bleu *very rare*
bleu d'auvergne *blue cheese from Auvergne*
bœuf bourguignon *beef cooked in red wine*
bœuf braisé *braised beef*
bœuf en daube *beef casserole*
bœuf miroton *beef and onion stew*
bœuf mode *beef stew with carrots*
bolet *boletus (mushroom)*
boudin blanc *white pudding*
boudin noir *black pudding*
bouillabaisse *fish soup*
bouilli *boiled*
bouillon *broth*
bouillon de légumes *vegetable stock*
bouillon de poule *chicken stock*
boulette *meatball*
bouquet rose *prawns*
bourride *fish soup*
brandade *cod in cream and garlic*
brioche *round roll*
brochet *pike*
brochette *kebab*
brugnon *nectarine*
brûlot *flambéed brandy*
brut *very dry*

C

cabillaud *cod*
café *coffee (black)*
café au lait *white coffee*
café complet *continental breakfast*
café crème *white coffee*
café glacé *iced coffee*
café liégeois *iced coffee with cream*
caille *quail*
calamar/calmar *squid*
calvados *apple brandy*

canapé *small open sandwich, canapé*
canard *duck*
canard laqué *Peking duck*
caneton *duckling*
cantal *white cheese from Auvergne*
câpres *capers*
carbonnade *beef cooked in beer*
cari *curry*
carotte *carrot*
carottes Vichy *carrots in butter and parsley*
carpe *carp*
carré d'agneau *rack of lamb*
carrelet *plaice*
carte *menu*
carte des vins *wine list*
casse-croûte *snacks*
cassis *blackcurrant*
cassoulet *bean, pork and duck casserole*
céleri/céleri rave *celeriac*
céleri en branches *celery*
cèpe *cep (mushroom)*
cerise *cherry*
cerises à l'eau de vie *cherries in brandy*
cervelle *brains*
chabichou *goat's and cow's milk cheese*
chablis *dry white wine from Burgundy*
champignon *mushroom*
champignon de Paris *white button mushroom*
chanterelle *chanterelle (mushroom)*
chantilly *whipped cream*
charcuterie *sausages, ham and pâtés; pork products*
charlotte *dessert with fruit, cream, and biscuits*
chausson aux pommes *apple turnover*
cheval *horse*
chèvre *goat's cheese*
chevreuil *venison*
chicorée *endive*
chocolat chaud *hot chocolate*
chocolat glacé *iced chocolate*
chou *cabbage*

chou à la crème *cream puff*
choucroute *sauerkraut with sausages and ham*
chou-fleur *cauliflower*
chou rouge *red cabbage*
choux de Bruxelles *Brussels sprouts*
cidre *cider*
cidre doux *sweet cider*
citron *lemon*
citron pressé *fresh lemon juice*
civet de lièvre *jugged hare*
clafoutis *baked batter pudding with fruit*
cochon de lait *suckling pig*
cocktail de crevettes *prawn cocktail*
cœur *heart*
coing *quince*
colin *hake*
compote *stewed fruit*
comté *hard cheese from the Jura*
concombre *cucumber*
confit de canard *duck preserved in fat*
confit d'oie *goose preserved in fat*
confiture *jam*
congre *conger eel*
consommé *clear meat or chicken soup*
coq au vin *chicken in red wine*
coque *cockle*
coquelet *cockerel*
coquilles Saint-Jacques *scallops in cream sauce*
côte de porc *pork chop*
côtelette *chop*
cotriade bretonne *fish soup from Brittany*
coulommiers *rich, soft cheese*
court-bouillon *stock*
crabe *crab*
crème *cream; creamy sauce or dessert; white (coffee)*
crème à la vanille *vanilla custard*
crème anglaise *custard*
crème chantilly *whipped cream*
crème d'asperges *cream of asparagus soup*
crème de bolets *cream of mushroom soup*
crème de volaille *cream of chicken soup*
crème d'huîtres *cream of oyster soup*
crème fouettée *whipped cream*
crème pâtissière *rich, creamy custard*
crème renversée *set custard*
crème vichyssoise *cold leek and potato soup*

crêpe *pancake*
crêpe à la crème de marron *pancake with chestnut cream*
crêpe à l'œuf *pancake with fried egg*
crêpe de froment *wheat pancake*
crêpes Suzette *pancakes flambéed with orange sauce*
crépinette *small sausage patty wrapped in fat*
cresson *cress*
crevette grise *shrimp*
crevette rose *prawn*
croque-madame *grilled cheese and ham sandwich with a fried egg*
croque-monsieur *grilled cheese and ham sandwich*
crottin de Chavignol *small goat's cheese*
crustacés *shellfish*
cuisses de grenouille *frogs' legs*

D

dartois *pastry with jam*
dégustation *wine tasting*
digestif *liqueur*
dinde *turkey*
doux *sweet*

E

eau minérale gazeuse *sparkling mineral water*
eau minérale plate *still mineral water*
échalote *shallot*
écrevisse *freshwater crayfish*
endive *chicory*
en papillote *baked in foil or paper*
entrecôte *rib steak*
entrecôte au poivre *peppered rib steak*
entrecôte maître d'hôtel *steak with butter and parsley*
entrée *starter*
entremets *dessert*
épaule d'agneau farcie *stuffed shoulder of lamb*
épinards en branches *leaf spinach*
escalope de veau milanaise *veal escalope with tomato sauce*
escalope panée *breaded escalope*
escargot *snail*
estouffade de bœuf *beef casserole*
estragon *tarragon*

F

faisan *pheasant*
farci *stuffed*
fenouil *fennel*
filet *fillet*
filet de bœuf Rossini *fillet of beef with foie gras*
filet de perche *perch fillet*
fine *fine brandy*
flageolets *kidney beans*
flan *custard tart*
foie de veau *veal liver*
foie gras *goose or duck liver preserve*
foies de volaille *chicken livers*
fonds d'artichaut *artichoke hearts*
fondue bourguignonne *meat fondue*
fondue savoyarde *cheese fondue*
fraise *strawberry*
fraise des bois *wild strawberry*
framboise *raspberry*
frisée *curly lettuce*
frit *deep-fried*
frites *chips*
fromage *cheese*
fromage blanc *cream cheese*
fromage de chèvre *goat's cheese*
fruits de mer *seafood*

G

galette *round, flat cake or savoury wholemeal crêpe*
garni *with potatoes and vegetables*
gâteau *cake*
gaufre *wafer; waffle*
gelée *jelly*
Gewürztraminer *dry white wine from Alsace*
gibier *game*
gigot d'agneau *leg of lamb*
girolle *chanterelle (mushroom)*
glace *ice cream*
goujon *gudgeon (fish)*
gratin *dish baked with milk, cheese, and cream*
gratin dauphinois *sliced potatoes baked in milk, cream, and cheese*
gratinée *baked onion soup*
grillé *grilled*
grondin *gurnard (fish)*
groseille rouge *redcurrant*

H

hachis parmentier *shepherd's pie*
hareng mariné *marinated herring*
haricots *beans*

haricots blancs *haricot beans*
haricots verts *green beans*
homard *lobster*
hors-d'œuvre *starter*
huître *oyster*

I, J

îles flottantes *floating islands*
  (soft meringue on custard)
infusion *herb tea*
jambon *ham*
jambon de Bayonne *smoked*
  and cured ham
julienne *soup with chopped*
  vegetables
jus de fruits *fruit juice*
jus de pomme *apple juice*
jus d'orange *orange juice*

K, L

kir *white wine with*
  blackcurrant liqueur
kirsch *cherry brandy*
lait *milk*
laitue *lettuce*
langouste *saltwater crayfish*
langoustine *Dublin Bay prawn*
lapereau *young rabbit*
lapin *rabbit*
lapin de garenne *wild rabbit*
lard *bacon*
légume *vegetable*
lentilles *lentils*
lièvre *hare*
limande *lemon sole*
livarot *strong, soft cheese from*
  the north of France
longe *loin*
lotte *monkfish*
loup au fenouil *bass with fenne*

M

macédoine de légumes
  mixed vegetables
mache *corn salad (leafy*
  vegetable)
mangue *mango*
maquereau *mackerel*
marc *grape brandy*
marcassin *young boar*
marchand de vin *in red*
  wine sauce
marron *chestnut*
massepain *marzipan*
menthe *peppermint*
menthe à l'eau *mint cordial*
  with water
menu du jour *today's menu*
menu gastronomique
  gourmet menu
menu touristique *tourist menu*

merlan *whiting*
millefeuille *custard slice*
millésime *vintage*
morille *morel (mushroom)*
morue *cod*
moules *mussels*
moules marinière *mussels in*
  white wine
mousseux *sparkling*
moutarde *mustard*
mouton *mutton*
mulet *mullet*
munster *strong cheese*
mûre *blackberry*
Muscadet *dry white wine*
myrtille *bilberry*

N

nature *plain*
navarin *mutton stew with*
  vegetables
navet *turnip*
noisette *hazelnut*
noisette d'agneau *medallion*
  of lamb
noix *nuts, walnuts*
nouilles *noodles*

O

œuf à la coque *boiled egg*
œuf dur *hard-boiled egg*
œuf mollet *soft-boiled egg*
œuf poché *poached egg*
œufs brouillés *scrambled eggs*
œuf sur le plat *fried egg*
oie *goose*
oignon *onion*
omelette au naturel *plain*
  omelette
omelette aux fines herbes
  herb omelette
omelette paysanne *omelette*
  with potatoes and bacon
orange pressée *fresh orange*
  juice
oseille *sorrel*
oursin *sea urchin*

P

pain *bread*
pain au chocolat *chocolate*
  croissant
palette de porc *shoulder of pork*
palourde *clam*
pamplemousse *grapefruit*
pastis *anise-flavoured alcoholic*
  drink
pâté de canard *duck pâté*
pâté de foie de volaille
  chicken liver pâté
pâte feuilletée *puff pastry*

pâtes *pasta*
pêche *peach*
perdreau *young partridge*
perdrix *partridge*
petite friture *whitebait*
petit pain *roll*
petit pois *peas*
petits fours *small pastries*
petit suisse *cream cheese*
pied de porc *pig's feet*
pigeonneau *young pigeon*
pignatelle *cheese fritter*
pilaf de mouton *rice dish with*
  mutton
pintade *guinea fowl*
piperade *dish of egg, tomatoes,*
  and peppers
pissaladière *Provençal dish*
  similar to pizza
pistache *pistachio*
plat du jour *dish of the day*
plateau de fromages *cheese*
  board
pochouse *fish casserole with*
  white wine
poire *pear*
poireau *leek*
poisson *fish*
poivre *pepper*
poivron *red/green pepper*
pomme *apple*
pomme de terre *potato*
pommes de terre à l'anglaise
  boiled potatoes
pommes de terre en robe de
  chambre/des champs
  baked potatoes
pommes de terre sautées
  fried potatoes
pommes frites *chips*
pommes paille *finely cut chips*
pommes vapeur *steamed*
  potatoes
porc *pork*
potage *soup*
potage bilibi *fish and oyster soup*
potage Crécy *carrot and rice*
  soup
potage cressonnière
  watercress soup
potage Esaü *lentil soup*
potage parmentier *leek and*
  potato soup
potage printanier *vegetable*
  soup
potage Saint-Germain *split*
  pea soup
potage velouté *creamy soup*
pot-au-feu *beef and vegetable*
  stew
potée *vegetable and meat stew*
Pouilly-Fuissé *dry white wine*
  from Burgundy
poule au pot *chicken and*

vegetable stew
poulet basquaise *chicken with ratatouille*
poulet chasseur *chicken with mushrooms and white wine*
poulet créole *chicken in white sauce with rice*
poulet rôti *roast chicken*
praire *clam*
provençale *with tomatoes, garlic and herbs*
prune *plum*
pruneau *prune*
pudding *plum pudding*
purée *mashed potatoes*

Q

quenelle *meat or fish dumpling*
queue de bœuf *oxtail*
quiche lorraine *egg, bacon, and cream tart*

R

raclette *Swiss dish of melted cheese*
radis *radish*
ragoût *stew*
raie *skate*
raie au beurre noir *skate fried in butter*
raifort *horseradish*
raisin *grape*
râpé *grated*
rascasse *scorpion fish*
ratatouille *stew of peppers, courgettes, aubergines, and tomatoes*
ravigote *herb dressing*
reblochon *strong cheese from Savoy*
rémoulade *mayonnaise dressing with herbs, mustard, and capers*
rigotte *small goat's cheese from Lyon*
rillettes *potted pork or goose meat*
ris de veau *veal sweetbread*
riz *rice*
riz pilaf *spicy rice with meat or seafood*
rognon *kidney*
roquefort *blue cheese*
rôti *roasted/joint of meat*
rouget *mullet*

S

sabayon *zabaglione (whipped egg yolk in Marsala wine)*
sablé *shortbread*
saignant *rare*
saint-honoré *cream puff cake*

saint-marcellin *goat's cheese*
salade composée *mixed salad*
salade russe *diced vegetables in mayonnaise*
salade verte *green salad*
salmis *game stew*
salsifis *oyster plant, salsify*
sanglier *wild boar*
sauce aurore *white sauce with tomato purée*
sauce béarnaise *thick sauce of eggs and butter*
sauce blanche *white sauce*
sauce gribiche *dressing with hard-boiled eggs*
sauce hollandaise *rich sauce of eggs, butter and vinegar, served with fish*
sauce Madère *Madeira sauce*
sauce matelote *wine sauce*
sauce Mornay *béchamel sauce with cheese*
sauce mousseline *hollandaise sauce with cream*
sauce poulette *sauce of mushrooms and egg yolks*
sauce ravigote *dressing with shallots and herbs*
sauce suprême *creamy sauce*
sauce tartare *mayonnaise with herbs and gherkins*
sauce veloutée *white sauce with egg yolks and cream*
sauce vinot *wine sauce*
saucisse *sausage*
saucisse de Francfort *frankfurter*
saucisse de Strasbourg *beef sausage*
saucisson *salami*
saumon *salmon*
saumon fumé *smoked salmon*
sauternes *sweet white wine*
savarin *rum baba*
sec *dry*
seiche *cuttlefish*
sel *salt*
service (non) compris *service (not) included*
service 12% inclus *12% service charge included*
sole bonne femme *sole in white wine and mushrooms*
sole meunière *floured sole fried in butter*
soupe *soup*
soupe au pistou *thick vegetable soup with basil*
steak au poivre *peppered steak*
steak frites *steak and chips*
steak haché *minced meat, minced beef*
steak tartare *raw minced beef with a raw egg*

sucre *sugar*
suprême de volaille *chicken in cream sauce*

T

tanche *tench (fish)*
tarte aux fraises *strawberry tart*
tarte aux pommes *apple tart*
tarte frangipane *almond cream tart*
tartelette *small tart*
tarte Tatin *baked apple dish*
tartine *bread and butter*
tendrons de veau *breast of veal*
terrine *pâté*
tête de veau *calf's head*
thé *tea*
thé à la menthe *mint tea*
thé au lait *tea with milk*
thé citron *lemon tea*
thon *tuna*
tomates farcies *stuffed tomatoes*
tome de Savoie *white cheese from Savoy*
tournedos *round beef steak*
tourte *covered pie*
tourteau *type of crab*
tripes à la mode de Caen *tripe in spicy vegetable sauce*
truite au bleu *poached trout*
truite aux amandes *trout with almonds*
truite meunière *trout in flour and fried in butter*

V, Y

vacherin *strong, soft cheese from the Jura*
vacherin glacé *ice cream meringue*
veau *veal*
velouté de tomate *cream of tomato soup*
vermicelle *vermicelli (very fine pasta)*
viande *meat*
vin *wine*
vinaigrette *French dressing*
vin blanc *white wine*
vin de pays *local wine*
vin de table *table wine*
vin rosé *rosé wine*
vin rouge *red wine*
volaille *poultry*
VSOP *mature brandy*
yaourt *yoghurt*

DICTIONARY
English to French

The gender of a singular French noun is indicated by the word for *the*: **le** and **la** (masculine and feminine). If these are abbreviated to **l'** in front of a vowel or the letter *h*, or if the noun is plural, indicated by **les,** then the gender is indicated by the abbreviations (m) or (f). French adjectives (adj) vary according to the gender and number of the word they describe; the masculine form is shown here. In most cases, you add an **-e** to the masculine form to make it feminine. Certain endings use a different rule: masculine adjectives that end in **-x** adopt an **-se** ending in the feminine form, while those that end in **-ien** change to **-ienne**. Some feminine adjectives that do not follow these rules are shown here and follow the abbreviation (fem). For the plural form, a (silent) **-s** is usually added.

A

a **un/une**
about: about sixteen **environ seize**
accelerator **l'accélérateur** (m)
accident **l'accident** (m)
accommodation **l'hébergement** (m)
accountant **le/la comptable**
ache **la douleur**
adaptor (plug) **la prise multiple;** (voltage) **l'adaptateur** (m)
address **l'adresse** (f)
adhesive **l'adhésif** (m)
admission charge **le prix d'entrée**
advance **l'avance** (f)
after **après**
afternoon **l'après-midi** (m)
aftershave **l'après-rasage** (m)
again **de nouveau**
against **contre**
agenda **l'ordre du jour** (m)
agent **l'agent** (m)
AIDS **SIDA**
air **l'air** (m)
air conditioning **la climatisation**
aircraft **l'avion** (m)
airline **la compagnie aérienne**
air mail **par avion**
air mattress **le matelas pneumatique**
airport **l'aéroport** (m)
airport bus **la navette (pour l'aéroport)**
aisle (supermarket) **rayon**
alarm clock **le réveil**
alcohol **l'alcool** (m)
Algeria **l'Algérie** (f)

Algerian **algérien(ne)**
all **tout;** *all the streets* **toutes les rues;** *that's all* **c'est tout**
allergic **allergique**
almost **presque**
alone **seul**
Alps **les Alpes** (f)
already **déjà**
always **toujours**
am: I am **je suis**
ambulance **l'ambulance** (f)
America **l'Amérique** (f)
American **américain(e)**
and **et**
Andorra **Andorre**
ankle **la cheville**
another (different) **un/une autre;** *another coffee, please* **encore un café, s'il vous plaît**
answering machine **le réponder**
antifreeze **l'antigel** (m)
antique shop **le magasin d'antiquités; l'antiquaire** (m)
antiseptic **l'antiseptique** (m)
apartment **l'appartement** (m)
aperitif **l'apéritif** (m)
appetite **l'appétit** (m)
apple **la pomme**
application form **le formulaire de demande**
appointment **le rendez-vous**
apricot **l'abricot** (m)
April **avril**
architecture **l'architecture** (f)
are: you are (singular informal) **tu es;** *we are* **nous sommes;** (plural; singular formal) **vous êtes;** *they are* **ils/elles sont**

arm **le bras**
armchair **le fauteuil**
arrival **l'arrivée** (f)
arrive **arriver**
art **l'art** (m)
art gallery **le musée d'art; la galerie d'art**
artist **l'artiste** (m)
as: as soon as possible **dès que possible**
ashtray **le cendrier**
asleep **endormi;** *he's asleep* **il dort**
aspirin **l'aspirine** (f)
asthmatic **asthmatique**
at: at the post office **à la poste;** *at the café* **au café;** *at 3 o'clock* **à 3 heures**
attic **le grenier**
attractive **attirant**
August **août**
aunt **la tante**
Australia **l'Australie** (f)
Australian **australien(ne)**
automatic **automatique**
autumn **l'automne** (m)
avocado **l'avocat** (m)
away: is it far away? **est-ce que c'est loin?;** *go away!* **allez-vous en!**
awful **affreux**
axe **la hache**
axle **l'essieu** (m)

B

baby **le bébé**
baby wipes **les lingettes** (f)
back (not front) **l'arrière** (m);** (body) **le dos;** *I'll come back tomorrow* **je reviendrai demain**
backpack **le sac à dos**

bacon le bacon; *bacon and eggs* des œufs au bacon
bad mauvais
baggage les bagages (m)
baggage check in l'enregistrement des bagages (m)
baggage claim la réclamation de bagages
bait l'appât (m)
bake cuire
bakery la boulangerie
balcony le balcon
bald chauve
ball *(football etc)* le ballon; *(tennis etc)* la balle
ballpoint pen le stylo-bille
banana la banane
band *(musicians)* le groupe
bandage le pansement, le bandage
bank la banque
banknote le billet
bar le bar;
barbecue le barbecue
barber's le coiffeur
bargain la affaire
basement le sous-sol
basin *(sink)* le lavabo
basket le panier
bath le bain; *(bathtub)* la baignoire; *to have a bath* prendre un bain
bathroom la salle de bains
battery *(car)* la batterie; *(torch)* la pile
be être
beach la plage
beans les haricots (m)
beard la barbe
beautiful beau, *(fem)* belle
because parce que
bed le lit
bed linen les draps (m)
bedroom la chambre
beef le bœuf
beer la bière
before avant
beginner le débutant, la débutante
beginners' slope la piste pour débutants
behind derrière
beige beige
Belgian belge
Belgium la Belgique
bell *(church)* la cloche; *(door)* la sonnette
below ... sous ...
belt la ceinture
beside à côté de

best: *the best* le meilleur
better mieux
between ... entre ...
bicycle la bicyclette, le vélo
big grand
bill l'addition (f)
bin liner le sac poubelle
bird l'oiseau (m)
birthday l'anniversaire (m); *happy birthday!* joyeux anniversaire!
biscuit le biscuit
bite *(by dog)* la morsure; *(by snake)* la piqûre, *(verb: dog)* insect; mordre; *(insect, snake)* piquer
bitter amer
black noir
blackberry la mûre
blackcurrant le cassis
blanket la couverture
bleach l'eau de Javel (f); *(verb)* décolorer
blind *(cannot see)* aveugle; *(window)* le store
blister l'ampoule (f)
blizzard la tempête de neige
blond *(adj)* blond
blood le sang
blood test la prise de sang
blouse le chemisier
blue bleu
boarding pass la carte d'embarquement
boat le bateau; *(smaller)* la barque
body le corps
boil *(verb)* bouillir
boiled bouilli
boiler le chauffe-eau
bolt *(on door)* le verrou; verrouiller *(verb)*
bone l'os (m); *(fish)* l'arête (f)
bonnet *(car)* le capot
book le livre; réserver *(verb)*
bookshop la librairie
boot *(footwear)* la botte; *(car)* le coffre
border la frontière
boring ennuyeux
born: *I was born in ...* je suis né(e) en ...
both les deux; *both of them* tous les deux; *both of us* nous deux; *both large and small* grand et petit à la fois
bottle la bouteille
bottle opener le décapsuleur, l'ouvre-bouteille (m)

bottom le fond; *(part of body)* le derrière
bowl le bol; *(animal)* la gamelle
box la boîte
box office *(theatre etc)* le bureau de location
boy le garçon
boyfriend le petit ami
bra le soutien-gorge
bracelet le bracelet
braces *(clothes)* les bretelles (f)
brake le frein; *(verb)* freiner
branch la branche
brandy le cognac
bread le pain
breakdown *(car)* la panne; *(nervous)* la dépression; *I've had a breakdown (car)* je suis tombé en panne
breakfast le petit déjeuner
breathe respirer
bricklayer le maçon
bridge le pont
briefcase l'attaché-case (m)
British britannique
Brittany la Bretagne
brochure la brochure
broken cassé; *broken leg* la jambe cassée; *broken down* en panne
brooch la broche
brother le frère
brown marron
bruise le bleu
brush la brosse; *(paintbrush)* le pinceau; *(broom)* le balai; *(verb)* brosser
Brussels Bruxelles
bucket le seau
budget le budget
builder le constructeur
building le bâtiment
bumper le pare-chocs
bunker le bunker
burglary le cambriolage
burn la brûlure; *(verb)* brûler
bus le bus
business les affaires (f); *it's none of your business* cela ne vous regarde pas
business card la carte de visite
bus station la gare routière
bus stop l'arrêt de bus (m)
busy *(occupied)* occupé; *(street)* animé
but mais
butcher's la boucherie
butter le beurre

button **le bouton**
buy **acheter**
by: by the window **près de la fenêtre;** *by Friday* **d'ici vendredi;** *by myself* **tout seul;** *written by* **écrit par**

C

cabbage **le chou**
cabinet **le placard**
cable car **le téléphérique**
cable TV **la télé cablée**
café **le café**
cage **la cage**
cake **le gâteau**
cake shop **la pâtisserie**
calculator **la calculette**
call: what's it called?
   comment est-ce que ça s'appelle?
camcorder **le caméscope**
camera **l'appareil-photo** (m)
camper van **le camping-car**
campfire **le feu de camp**
campsite **le terrain de camping**
camshaft **l'arbre à cames** (m)
can (vessel) **la boîte de conserve;** (to be able) **pouvoir;** *can I have ...?* **Je peux avoir ...?;** *can you ...?* **Vous pouvez ...?**
Canada **le Canada**
Canadian **canadien(ne)**
canal **le canal**
candle **la bougie**
canoe **le canoë**
can opener **l'ouvre-boîte** (m)
cap (hat) **la casquette;** (bottle) **la capsule**
car **la voiture;** (train) **la voiture, le wagon**
caravan **la caravane**
carburettor **le carburateur**
card **la carte**
cardigan **le gilet**
careful **prudent;** *careful!* **attention!;** *be careful!* **soyez prudent!**
caretaker **le/la concierge**
car park **le parking**
carpenter **le charpentier**
carpet **le tapis**
carriage (train) **la voiture**
carrot **la carotte**
car seat (for a baby) **le siège pour bébé**
case **la valise**
cash **l'argent** (m); *to pay cash* **payer en liquide**

cashier **le guichet**
cash machine **le distributeur automatique**
cassette **la cassette**
cassette player **le lecteur de cassettes**
castle **le château**
cat **le chat**
cathedral **la cathédrale**
cauliflower **le chou-fleur**
cave **la grotte**
ceiling **le plafond**
cellar **la cave**
cemetery **le cimetière**
central heating **le chauffage central**
centre **le centre**
certificate **le certificat**
chair **la chaise**
change (money) **la monnaie;** (verb: money) **changer;** (clothes) **se changer**
Channel **la Manche**
Channel Islands **les îles Anglo-Normandes**
Channel Tunnel **le tunnel sous la Manche**
charger **le chargeur**
cheap **bon marché, pas cher**
check-in **l'enregistrement** (m)
check in **faire enregistrer ses bagages**
check-out (supermarket) **la caisse**
cheers! (toast) **santé!**
cheese **le fromage**
cheese shop **la fromagerie**
chemist's **la pharmacie**
cheque **le chèque**
chequebook **le carnet de chèques**
cherry **la cerise**
chess **les échecs** (m)
chest **la poitrine**
chest of drawers **la commode**
chicken **le poulet**
child **l'enfant** (m)
children **les enfants** (m)
children's ward **le service de pédiatrie**
chimney **la cheminée**
china **la porcelaine**
chips **les frites** (f)
chocolate **le chocolat;** *a box of chocolates* **la boîte de chocolats;** *chocolate bar* **la tablette de chocolat**
chop (food) **la côtelette;** **couper** (verb: cut)
church **l'église** (f)

cigar **le cigare**
cigarette **la cigarette**
cinema **le cinéma**
city **la ville**
city centre **le centre ville**
class **la classe**
classical music **la musique classique**
clean (adj) **propre**
cleaner **la femme de ménages**
clear **clair**
clever **intelligent**
clock **l'horloge** (f), **la pendule**
close **près** (near); **étouffant** (stuffy); **fermer** (verb)
closed **fermé**
clothes **les vêtements** (m)
clubs (cards) **trèfle**
clutch **l'embrayage** (m)
coat **le manteau**
coat hanger **le cintre**
cockroach **le cafard**
cocktail party **le cocktail**
coffee **le café;** *white coffee* **café crème**
coin **la pièce**
cold (illness) **le rhume;** **froid** (adj)
collar **le col, le collier**
collection (stamps etc) **la collection;** (postal) **la levée**
colour **la couleur**
colour film **la pellicule couleur**
comb **le peigne;** (verb) **peigner**
come **venir;** *I come from ...* **je viens de ...;** *we came last week* **nous sommes arrivés la semaine dernière**
compact disc **le disque compact**
company **la compagnie**
compartment **le compartiment**
complicated **compliqué**
computer **l'ordinateur** (m)
computer games **les jeux vidéos** (m)
concert **le concert**
conditioner (hair) **le baume après-shampooing**
condom **le préservatif**
conductor (orchestra) **le chef d'orchestre**
confectioner **le confiseur**
conference **la conférence**

conference room **la salle de conférences**
congratulations! **félicitations!**
consulate **le consulat**
consultant **consultant(e)**
contact lenses **les verres de contact** (f)
contraceptive **le contraceptif**
cook **le cuisinier; faire la cuisine** (verb)
cooker **la cuisinière**
cooking utensils **les utensiles de cuisine** (f)
cool **frais, (fem) fraîche**
cork **le bouchon**
corkscrew **le tire-bouchon**
corner **le coin**
corridor **le couloir**
Corsica **la Corse**
Corsican **corse**
cosmetics **les produits de beauté** (m)
cost (verb) **coûter;** *how much does it cost?* **combien ça coûte?**
cot **le lit d'enfant**
cotton **le coton**
cotton balls **le coton hydrophile**
cough **la toux;** (verb) **tousser**
country (state) **le pays;** (not town) **la campagne**
courgette **la courgette**
cousin **le cousin**
crab **le crabe**
cramp **la crampe**
crayfish (freshwater) **l'écrevisse** (f); (saltwater) **la langouste**
cream **la crème**
credit card **la carte de crédit**
crisps **les chips** (f)
cross over (verb) **traverser**
crowded **bondé**
cruise **la croisière**
crutches **les béquilles** (f)
cry (weep) **pleurer;** (shout) **crier**
cucumber **le concombre**
cuff links **les boutons de manchette** (m)
cup **la tasse**
curlers **les rouleaux** (m)
curls **les boucles** (f)
current **le courant**
curry **le curry**
curtain **le rideau**
customs **la douane**
cut **la coupure;** (verb) **couper**
cycling **le vélo**

D

dad **papa**
dairy products **les produits laitiers** (m)
dance **la danse;** (verb) **danser**
dangerous **dangereux**
dark **foncé;** *dark blue* **bleu foncé**
daughter **la fille**
day **le jour**
dead **mort**
deaf **sourd**
dear **cher**
debit card **la carte bancaire**
December **décembre**
decorator **le décorateur**
deep **profond**
delay **le retard**
deliberately **exprès**
delicatessen **la charcuterie**
delivery **la livraison**
dentist **le/la dentiste**
dentures **le dentier**
deny **nier**
deodorant **le déodorant**
department **la département**
department store **le grand magasin**
departures (airport etc) **le départ**
designer **le designer**
desk **le bureau**
desserts **les desserts** (m)
develop **développer**
diabetic **diabétique**
diamond (jewel) **le diamant**
diamonds (cards) **carreau**
diarrhoea **la diarrhée**
diary **l'agenda** (m)
dictionary **le dictionnaire**
die **mourir**
diesel **le diesel; le gazoile**
different **différent;** *that's different* **c'est différent;** *I'd like a different one* **j'en voudrais un autre**
difficult **difficile**
dining room **la salle à manger**
dinner **le dîner**
dinner party **le dîner**
directory (telephone) **l'annuaire** (m); **les reseignments** (m)
disabled **handicapé**
disco **le discothèque**
discount **la réduction**
dish cloth **le torchon**
dishwasher **le lave-vaisselle**
disposable nappies **les couches à jeter** (f)

distributor (car) **le delco**
dive (verb) **plonger**
diving board **le plongeoir**
divorced **divorcé**
do **faire;** *how do you do?* **comment allez-vous?**
dock **le quai**
doctor **le docteur; médecin**
document **le document**
dog **le chien**
doll **la poupée**
dollar **le dollar**
door (building) **la porte;** (car) **la portière**
double room **la chambre pour deux personnes**
doughnut **le beignet**
down **en bas**
drawer **le tiroir**
drawing pin **la punaise**
dress **la robe**
drink **la boisson;** (verb) **boire;** *would you like a drink?* **vous voulez boire quelque chose?**
drinking water **l'eau potable** (f)
drive (verb: car) **conduire**
driver **le conducteur**
driveway **le passage**
driving licence **le permis de conduire**
drops **les goutes** (f)
drunk **soûl, ivre**
dry **sec, (fem) sèche**
dry cleaner's **le pressing**
during **pendant**
duster **le chiffon à poussière**
duty-free **hors-taxe**
duvet **la couette**

E

each (every) **chaque;** *two euros each* **deux euros pièce**
ear **l'oreille** (f)
early **tôt**
earrings **les boucles d'oreille** (f)
east **l'est** (m)
easy **facile**
eat **manger**
egg **l'œuf** (m)
eight **huit**
eighteen **dix-huit**
eighty **quatre-vingt**
either: *either of them* **n'importe lequel;** *either ... or ...* **soit ... soit ...**
elastic **élastique**
elastic band **l'élastique** (m)

elbow le coude
electric électrique
electrician électricien(ne)
electricity l'électricité (f)
eleven onze
else: something else autre chose; *someone else* quelqu'un d'autre; *somewhere else* ailleurs
e-mail l'email (m), le message, la messagerie électronique
e-mail address l'adresse électronique (f)
embarrassing gênant
embassy l'ambassade (f)
embroidery la broderie
emerald l'émeraude (f)
emergency l'urgence (f)
emergency departement la salle des urgences
emergency exit la sortie de secours
empty vide
end la fin
engaged (couple) fiancé
engine (car) le moteur; (train) la locomotive
engineer l'ingénieur (m)
engineering l'ingénierie (f)
England l'Angleterre (f)
English anglais(e)
enlargement l'agrandissement (m)
enough assez
entertainment le divertissement
entrance l'entrée (f)
envelope l'enveloppe (f)
epileptic épileptique
eraser la gomme
escalator l'escalier roulant (m)
especially particulièrement
estimate l'estimation (f)
evening le soir
every chaque
everyone tout le monde
everything tout
everywhere partout
example l'exemple (m); *for example* par exemple
excellent excellent
excess baggage l'excédent de bagages (m)
exchange (verb) échanger
exchange rate le taux de change
excursion l'excursion (f)
excuse me! pardon!
executive (in company) cadre (m)

exhaust (car) le pot d'echappement
exhibition l'exposition (f)
exit la sortie
expensive cher
extension lead la rallonge
exterior l'extérieure (m); extérieure (adj)
eye l'œil (m)
eyebrow le sourcil
eyes les yeux (m)

F

face le visage
faint vague; *to faint* evanouir
fair la foire; (just) juste; *it's not fair* ce n'est pas juste
fan (ventilator) le ventilateur; (enthusiast) le/la fan
fan belt la courroie du ventilateur
fantastic fantastique
far loin; *how far is it to ...?* est-ce que ... est loin d'ici?
fare le prix du billet
farm la ferme
farmer le fermier
fashion la mode
fast rapide
fat (of person) gros, (fem) grosse; (on meat etc) le gras
father le père
fax le fax; (verb: document) faxer
fax machine le fax
February fevrier
feel (touch) toucher; *I feel hot* j'ai chaud; *I feel like ...* j'ai envie de ...; *I don't feel well* je ne me sens pas bien
feet les pieds (m)
felt-tip pen le feutre
ferry (small) le bac; (large) le ferry
fever la fièvre
fiancé le fiancé
fiancée la fiancée
field le champ; (academic) secteur (m)
fifteen quinze
fifty cinquante
fig la figue
figures les chiffres (m)
filling (in tooth) le plombage; (in sandwich, cake) la garniture
film le film

filter paper le papier filtre
finger le doigt
fire le feu; (blaze) l'incendie (m)
fire extinguisher l'extincteur (m)
fireplace la cheminée
fireworks le feu d'artifice
first premier
first aid les premiers soins (m)
first class première classe
first floor le premier étage
first name le prénom
fish le poisson
fishing la pêche; *to go fishing* aller à la pêche
fishing rod la canne à pêche
fishmonger's la poissonnerie
five cinq
fizzy water l'eau gazeuse (f)
flag le drapeau
flash (camera) le flash
flat (level) plat
flat tyre le pneu crevé
flavour le goût
flea la puce
flight le vol
flight attendant l'hôtesse de l'air (f)
flip-flops les tongs (f)
flippers les palmes (f)
floor (ground) le plancher; (storey) l'étage (m)
florist la fleuriste
flour la farine
flower la fleur
flowerbed le parterre de fleurs
flute la flûte
fly (insect) la mouche; (verb: of plane etc) voler; (of person) prendre l'avion
fog le brouillard
folk music la musique folklorique
food la nourriture
food poisoning l'intoxication alimentaire (f)
foot le pied
football le football
for pour; *for me* pour moi; *what for?* pour quoi faire?; *for a week* pour une semaine
foreigner l'étranger (m)
forest la forêt
forget oublier
fork la fourchette
fortnight quinze jours
forty quarante
fountain pen le stylo-plume

four **quatre**
fourteen **quatorze**
fourth **quatrième**
France **la France**
free (no cost) **gratuit**; (at liberty) **libre**
freezer **le congélateur**
French **français(e)**
Friday **vendredi**
fridge **le frigo**
fried **frit**
friend **l'ami(e)**
friendly **amical, gentil**
fringe **la frange**
front: in front **devant**
frost **le gel**
frozen foods **les produits surgelés** (m)
fruit **le fruit**
fruit juice **le jus de fruit**
fry **frire**
frying pan **la poêle**
full **complet**; *I'm full!* **j'ai l'estomac bien rempli!**
full board **la pension complète**
funny **drôle**
furnished **meublé**
furniture **les meubles** (m)

G

garage **le garage**
garden **le jardin**
garden centre **la jardinerie**
garlic **l'ail** (m)
gas **le gaz**
gas-permeable lenses **les lentilles semi-souples** (f)
gate **le portail, la grille**; (at airport) **la porte d'embarquement**
gay **homosexuel**
gear (car) **la vitesse**
gearbox **la boîte de vitesses**
gearstick **le levier de vitesse**
gel **le gel**
German **allemand(e)**
Germany **l'Allemagne** (f)
get (fetch) **aller chercher**; *have you got ...?* **avez-vous ...?**; *to get the train* **prendre le train**; *get back: we get back tomorrow* **nous rentrons demain**; *to get something back* **récupérer quelque chose**
get in **entrer**; (arrive) **arriver**
get off (bus etc) **descendre**
get on (bus etc) **monter**
get out **sortir**

get up **se lever**
gift **le cadeau**
gin **le gin**
ginger **le gingembre**
girl (child) **la fille**; (young woman) **la jeune fille**
girlfriend **la petite amie**
give **donner**
glad **heureux**
glass **le verre**
glasses **les lunettes** (f)
gloves **les gants** (m)
glue **la colle**
go **aller**
gold **l'or** (m)
golf **le golf**
golf course **le parcours de golf**
good **bon**, (fem) **bonne**; *good!* **bien!**
goodbye **au revoir**
good evening **bonsoir**
government **le gouvernement**
granddaughter **la petite-fille**
grandfather **le grand-père**
grandmother **la grand-mère**
grandparents **les grands-parents** (m)
grandson **le petit-fils**
grapes **les raisins** (m)
grass **l'herbe** (f)
Great Britain **la Grande-Bretagne**
green **vert**
grey **gris**
grill **le gril**
grilled **grillé(e)**
grocer's **l'épicerie** (f)
ground floor **le rez-de-chaussée**
groundsheet **le tapis de sol**
guarantee **la garantie**; (verb) **garantir**
guard (train) **le chef de train**
guest **l'invité(e)**
guide **le/la guide**
guide book **le guide**
guitar **la guitare**
gun (rifle) **le fusil**; (pistol) **le pistolet**
gutter **la gouttière**

H

hair **les cheveux** (m); *long/short hair* **les cheveux longs/courts**
haircut **la coupe (de cheveux)**
hairdresser **le coiffeur**

hairdryer **le sèche-cheveux**
hairspray **la laque**
half **demi**; *half an hour* **une demi-heure**
half board **la demi-pension**
ham **le jambon**
hamburger **le hamburger**
hammer **le marteau**
hamster **le hamster**
hand **la main**
hand luggage **le bagage à main**
handbag **le sac à main**
handbrake **le frein à main**
handkerchief **le mouchoir**
handle (door) **la poignée**
handsome **beau**
hangover **la gueule de bois**
happy **heureux**
harbour **le port**
hard **dur**; (difficult) **difficile**
hard lenses **les lentilles rigides** (f)
hardware shop **la quincaillerie**
hat **le chapeau**
have **avoir**; *have you got ...?* **avez-vous ...?**
hay fever **le rhume des foins**
he **il**
head **la tête**
head office **le siège social**
headache **le mal à la tête**
headlights **les phares** (m)
headphones **les écouteurs** (m)
hear **entendre**
hearing aid **l'appareil acoustique**
heart **le cœur**
heart condition **le problème au cœur**
hearts (cards) **cœurs**
heater **le radiateur**
heating **le chauffage**
heavy **lourd**
hedge **la haie**
heel **le talon**
hello **bonjour**
help **l'aide** (f); (verb) **aider**
hepatitis **l'hépatite** (f)
her: it's for her **c'est pour elle**; *give it to her* **donnez-le lui**
her: her book **son livre**; *her house* **sa maison**; *her shoes* **ses chaussures**; *it's hers* **c'est à elle**
hi **salut**
high **haut**
highway code **le code de la route**

hiking **la randonée**
hill **la colline**
him: it's for him **c'est pour lui;** *give it to him* **donnez-le lui**
his: his book **son livre;** *his house* **sa maison;** *his shoes* **ses chaussures;** *it's his* **c'est à lui**
history **l'histoire** (f)
hitchhike **faire de l'autostop**
HIV positive **séropositif(ve)**
hobby **le passe-temps**
holiday **les vacances** (f)
home: at home (my home) **chez moi;** *he's at home* **il est chez lui**
homeopathy **homéopathie**
honest **honnête**
honey **le miel**
honeymoon **la lune de miel**
horn (car) **le klaxon;** (animal) **la corne**
horrible **horrible**
hospital **l'hôpital** (m)
host **l'hôte** (m)
hostess **l'hôtesse** (f)
hot **chaud**
hotel **l'hôtel** (m)
hour **l'heure** (f)
house **la maison**
household products **les produits entretien** (m)
hovercraft **l'aéroglisseur** (m)
hoverport **l'hoverport** (m)
how? **comment?**
how much? **combien?**
hundred **cent**
hungry: I'm hungry **j'ai faim**
hurry: I'm in a hurry **je suis pressé**
husband **le mari**
hydrofoil **l'hydrofoil** (m)

I

I **je**
ice **la glace**
ice cream **la glace**
ice rink **la patinoire**
ice skates **les patins à glace** (m)
ice-skating: to go ice-skating **aller patiner**
identification **la identification**
if **si**
ignition **l'allumage** (m)

ill **malade**
immediately **immédiatement**
impossible **impossible**
in **dans;** *in France* **en France**
indicator **le clignotant**
indigestion **l'indigestion** (f)
inexpensive **bon marché, pas cher**
infection **l'infection** (f)
information **l'information** (f)
injection **la piqûre**
injury **la blessure**
ink **l'encre** (f)
inn **l'auberge** (f)
inner tube **la chambre à air**
insect **l'insecte** (m)
insect repellent **la crème anti-insecte**
insomnia **l'insomnie** (f)
instant coffee **le café soluble**
insurance **l'assurance** (f)
interesting **intéressant**
internet **l'internet** (m)
interpret **interpréter**
interpreter **l'interprète** (m)
invitation **l'invitation** (f)
invoice **la facture**
Ireland **l'Irlande** (f)
Irish **irlandais(e)**
iron (for clothes) **le fer à repasser;** (verb) **repasser**
is: he/she is **il/elle est;** *it is* **c'est**
island **l'île** (f)
it **il; elle**
Italian **italien(ne)**
Italy **l'Italie** (f)
its **son; sa; ses** (see his)

J

jacket **la veste**
jam **la confiture**
January **janvier**
jazz **le jazz**
jeans **les jeans** (m)
jellyfish **la méduse**
jeweller's **la bijouterie**
job **le travail**
jog (verb) **faire du jogging;** *to go for a jog* **aller faire du jogging**
joke **la plaisanterie**
journey **le voyage**
July **juillet**
June **juin**
just: it's just arrived **ça vient juste d'arriver;** *I've just one left* **il ne m'en reste qu'un**

K

kettle **la bouilloire**
key **la clé**
keyboard **le clavier**
kidney **le rein**
kilo **le kilo**
kilometre **le kilomètre**
kind **gentil**
kitchen **la cuisine**
knee **le genou**
knife **le couteau**
knit **tricoter**
knitting needle **l'aiguille à tricoter** (f)
know (fact) **savoir;** (person) **connaître;** *I don't know* **je ne sais pas**

L

label **l'étiquette** (f)
lace **la dentelle;** (of shoe) **le lacet**
lake **le lac**
lamb **l'agneau** (m)
lamp **la lampe**
lampshade **l'abat-jour** (m)
land **la terre;** (verb) **atterrir**
language **la langue**
laptop **l'ordinateur portable** (m)
large **grand**
last (final) **dernier;** *last week* **la semaine dernière;** *at last!* **enfin!**
late **tard;** *the bus is late* **le bus est en retard**
later **plus tard**
laugh **rire**
launderette **la laverie automatique**
laundry (place) **la blanchisserie;** (clothes) **le linge**
law (subject) **le droit**
lawn **la pelouse**
lawn mower **la tondeuse à gazon**
lawyer **avocat(e)**
laxative **le laxatif**
lazy **paresseux**
lead **la laisse**
leaf **la feuille**
leaflet **le dépliant**
learn **apprendre**
leather **le cuir**
lecture theatre **l'amphithéâtre** (m)
leek **le poireaux**

left (not right) **la gauche**; *there's nothing left* **il ne reste plus rien**
leg **la jambe**
lemon **le citron**
lemonade **la limonade**
length **la longueur**
lens (camera) **l'objectif** (m)
less **moins**
lesson **la leçon**
letter **la lettre**
lettuce **la salade**
library **la bibliothèque**
licence **le permis**
life **la vie**
lift **l'ascenseur** (m)
light **la lumière**; (not heavy) **léger**; (not dark) **clair**
light bulb **l'ampoule** (f)
lighter **le briquet**
lighter fluid **le gaz à briquet**
light meter **la cellule photoélectrique**
like (verb) **aimer**: *I like swimming* **j'aime nager**; *I don't like* **je n'aime pas**; (similar to) **comme**
lime (fruit) **le citron vert**
lipstick **le rouge à lèvres**
liqueur **la liqueur**
list **la liste**
literature **la littérature**
litre **le litre**
litter **les ordures** (f)
little (small) **petit**; *it's a little big* **c'est un peu trop grand**; *just a little* **juste un peu**
liver **le foie**
living room **le salon**
lobster **le homard**
lollipop **la sucette**
long **long**, (fem) **longue**
lost property **les objets trouvés** (m)
loud **fort**; (colour) **criard**
love **l'amour** (m); (verb) **aimer**
lover **l'amant** (m)
low **bas**
luck **la chance**; *good luck!* **bonne chance!**
luggage **les bagages** (m)
luggage lockers **la consigne automatique**
luggage rack **le porte-bagages**
lunch **le déjeuner**
Luxembourg **le Luxembourg**

M

mad **fou**, (fem) **folle**
magazine **la revue**
maid **la femme de chambre**
main courses **les plats** (m)
make **faire**
make-up **le maquillage**
man **l'homme** (m)
manager **le directeur**; **le chef**
many **beaucoup**; *not many* **pas beaucoup**
map **la carte**; (town map) **le plan**
March **mars**
margarine **la margarine**
market **le marché**
marmalade **la marmelade d'oranges**
married **marié**
mascara **le mascara**
mass (church) **la messe**
mast **le mât**
match (light) **l'allumette** (f); (sport) **le match**
material (cloth) **le tissu**
matter: *it doesn't matter* **ça ne fait rien**
mattress **le matelas**
May **mai**
maybe **peut-être**
me: *it's me* **c'est moi**; *it's for me* **c'est pour moi**; *give it to me* **donnez-le-moi**
meal **le repas**
mean: *what does this mean?* **qu'est-ce que cela veut dire?**
meat **la viande**
mechanic **le mécanicien**, **le garagiste**
medication **les médicaments** (m)
medicine **le médicament**; (subject) **le médicine**
Mediterranean **la Méditerranée**
meeting **la réunion**
melon **le melon**
menu **la carte**; *set menu* **le menu**
message **le message**
microwave **le micro-ondes**
middle **le milieu**
midnight **minuit**
milk **le lait**
mine: *it's mine* **c'est à moi**
mineral water **l'eau minérale** (f)

minute **la minute**
mirror **le miroir**; (car) **le rétroviseur**
Miss **Mademoiselle**
mistake **l'erreur** (f)
mobile phone **le téléphone portable**
modem **le modem**
Monday **lundi**
money **l'argent** (m)
monitor (computer) **le moniteur**
month **le mois**
monument **le monument**
moon **la lune**
moped **la mobylette**
more **plus**; *more or less* **plus ou moins**
morning **le matin**; *in the morning* **dans la matinée**
mosquito **le moustique**
mother **la mère**
motorboat **le bateau à moteur**
motorcycle **la moto**
motorway **l'autoroute** (f)
mountain **la montagne**
mountain bike **le vélo tout terrain**
mouse **la souris**
mousse (hair) **la mousse**
moustache **la moustache**
mouth **la bouche**
move **bouger**; (house) **déménager**; *don't move!* **ne bougez pas!**
Mr **Monsieur**
Mrs **Madame**
mug **la tasse**
museum **le musée**
mushroom **le champignon**
music **la musique**
musical instrument **l'instrument de musique** (m)
musician **le musicien**
mussels **les moules** (f)
must: *I must* **je dois**
mustard **la moutarde**
my: *my book* **mon livre**; *my house* **ma maison**; *my shoes* **mes chaussures**

N

nail (metal) **le clou**; (finger) **l'ongle** (m)
nail clippers **la pince à ongles**
nailfile **la lime à ongles**

nail polish **le vernis à ongles**
name **le nom;** *what's your name* **comment vous appelez-vous?**
nappy **la couche**
narrow **étroit**
near: near the door **près de la porte**
necessary **nécessaire**
neck **le cou**
necklace **le collier**
need (verb) **avoir besoin de;** *I need ...* **j'ai besoin de ...;** *there's no need* **ce n'est pas nécessaire**
needle **l'aiguille** (f)
negative (photo) **le négatif**
neither: neither of them **ni l'un ni l'autre;** *neither ...* *nor ...* **ni ... ni ...**
nephew **le neveu**
never **jamais**
new **nouveau,** (fem) **nouvelle; neuf,** (fem) **neuve**
news **les nouvelles** (f); (television) **les informations** (f)
newsagent's **le tabac;** **le tabac-journaux**
newspaper **le journal**
next **prochain;** *next week* **la semaine prochaine;** *what next?* **et puis quoi?**
nice (place etc) **joli;** (person) **sympathique**
niece **la nièce**
night **la nuit**
nightclub **la boîte de nuit**
nightdress **la chemise de nuit**
nine **neuf**
nineteen **dix-neuf**
ninety **quatre-vingt-dix**
no (response) **non;** (not any) **aucun**
nobody **personne**
noisy **bruyant**
none **aucun**
noon **midday**
north **le nord**
nose **le nez**
not **pas;** *he's not ...* **il n'est pas ...**
notebook **le carnet**
notepad **le bloc notes**
nothing **rien**
novel **le roman**
November **novembre**

now **maintenant**
nowhere **nulle part**
nudist **le nudiste**
number (figure) **le numéro;** (amount) **le nombre**
number plate **la plaque d'immatriculation**
nurse **infirmier;** (fem) **infirmière**
nut (fruit) **la noix;** (for bolt) **l'écrou** (m)

O

oars **les rames** (f)
occasionally **de temps en temps**
October **octobre**
of **de**
of course **bien sûr**
office **le bureau**
often **souvent**
oil **l'huile** (f)
ointment **la pommade**
OK **d'accord**
old **vieux,** (fem) **vieille;** *how old are you?* **quel âge avez-vous?**
olive **l'olive** (f)
omelette **l'omelette** (f)
on ... **sur ...**
one **un/une**
onion **l'oignon** (m)
only **seulement**
open **ouvert** (adj); (verb) **ouvrir**
opening times **les heures d'ouverture** (f)
operating theatre **la salle d'opérations**
operation **l'opération** (f)
operator (phone) **l'opérateur** (m)
opposite **en face de**
optician's **l'opticien** (m)
or **ou**
orange (fruit) **l'orange** (f); (colour) **orange**
orange juice **le jus d'orange**
orchestra **l'orchestre** (m)
ordinary **habituel**
organ (music) **l'orgue** (m)
other: the other ... **l'autre ...**
our: our house **notre maison;** *our children* **nos enfants;** *it's ours* **c'est à nous**
out: he's out **il n'est pas là**
outside **dehors**
oven **le four**

over (above) **au-dessus de;** (more than) **plus de;** (finished) **fini;** *it's over the road* **c'est de l'autre côté de la rue;** *over there* **là-bas**
overtake (in a car) **doubler**
oyster **l'huître** (f)

P

pack of cards **le jeu de cartes**
package **le paquet;** (parcel) **le colis**
packet **le paquet**
padlock **le cadenas**
page **la page**
pain **la douleur**
paint **la peinture**
painting **la peinture**
pair **la paire**
palace **le palais**
pale **pâle, blême**
pancake **la crêpe**
paper **le papier;** (newspaper) **le journal**
paraffin **le pétrole**
parcel **le colis**
pardon? **pardon?**
parents **les parents** (m)
park **le jardin public;** (verb) **garer**
parting (in hair) **la raie**
party (celebration) **la fête, la soirée;** (group) **le groupe;** (political) **le parti**
passenger **le passager**
passport **le passeport**
passport control **le contrôle des passeports**
password **le mot de passe**
pasta **les pâtes** (f)
path **le chemin, l'allée** (f)
pavement **le trottoir**
pay **payer**
payment **le paiement**
peach **la pêche**
peanuts **les cacahuètes** (f)
pear **la poire**
pearl **la perle**
peas **les petits pois** (m)
pedestrian **le piéton**
peg **la pince à linge**
pen **le stylo**
pencil **le crayon**
pencil sharpener **le taille-crayon**
penknife **le canif**
pen pal **le correspondant**
people **les gens** (m)

pepper (and salt) le poivre;
(red/green) le poivron
peppermints les bonbons
à la menthe (m)
per: per night par nuit
perfect parfait
perfume le parfum
perhaps peut-être
perm la permanente
pet passport le passeport
d'animaux
petrol l'essence (f)
petrol station la
station-service
pets les animaux
(familiers) (m)
phonecard la carte
téléphonique
photocopier le copieur
photograph la photo; (verb)
photographier
photographer le/la
photographe
phrase book le guide
de conversation
piano le piano
pickpocket le pickpocket
picnic le pique-nique
piece le morceau
pill le comprimé
pillow l'oreiller (m)
pilot le pilote
PIN le code
pin l'épingle (f)
pineapple l'ananas (m)
pink rose
pipe (for smoking) la pipe;
(for water) le tuyau
piston le piston
pitch l'emplacement (m)
pizza la pizza
place l'endroit (m); at your
place chez vous
plant la plante
plaster le pansement
plastic le plastique
plastic bag le sac
plastic wrap le film
alimentaire transparent
plate l'assiette (f)
platform le quai
play (theatre) la pièce; (verb)
jouer
please s'il vous plaît
pleased: pleased to meet you
enchanté(e)
plug (electrical) la prise;
(sink) le bouchon
plumber (occupation) le
plombier
pocket la poche

poison le poison
police la police
police officer le policier
police report le rapport de
police
police station le commissariat
politics la politique
poor pauvre; (bad quality)
mauvais
pop music la musique pop
pork le porc
port (harbour) le port; (drink)
le porto
porter le porteur
possible possible
post la poste; (verb) poster
postbox la boîte à lettres
postcard la carte postale
postcode le code postal
poster (outside) l'affiche (f);
(inside) le poster
postman le facteur
post office la poste
potato la pomme de terre
poultry la volaille
pound (money, weight) la livre
powder la poudre
pram le landau
prefer préférer
prescription l'ordonnance (f)
pretty (beautiful) joli; (quite)
plutôt
price le prix
priest le prêtre
printer l'imprimante (f)
private privé
problem le problème
profession la profession
professor le professeur
profits les bénéfices (m)
public le public
pull tirer
puncture la crevaison
purple violet
purse le porte-monnaie
push pousser
pushchair la poussette
put mettre
pyjamas le pyjama

Q

quality la qualité
quarter le quart
question la question
queue la queue; (verb)
faire la queue
quick rapide
quiet (preson) silencieux;
(street, etc) tranquille
quite (fairly) assez; (fully) très

R

rabbit le lapin
radiator le radiateur
radio la radio
radish le radis
rail: by rail par chemin
de fer
railway le chemin de fer
rain la pluie
raincoat l'imperméable (m)
raisin le raisin sec
rake le râteau
rare (uncommon) rare; (steak)
saignant
rash la rougeur
raspberry la framboise
rat le rat
razor blades les lames de
rasoir (f)
read lire
reading lamp la lampe de
bureau; (bedside) la
lampe de chevet
ready prêt
ready meals les plats
préparés (m)
receipt le reçu
reception la réception
receptionist le/la
receptionniste
record (music) le disque;
(sports etc) le record
record player le
tourne-disque
record shop le disquaire
red rouge; (hair) roux
refreshments les
rafraîchissements (m)
registered post en
recommandé
relax se détendre
religion la religion
remember: I remember je
m'en souviens; I don't
remember je ne me
souviens pas
rent (verb) louer
reservation la réservation
reserve (verb) réserver
rest (remainder) le reste;
(verb: relax) se reposer
restaurant le restaurant
restaurant car le
wagon-restaurant
return (come back) revenir;
(give back) rendre
return ticket l'aller retour
(m)
rice le riz
rich riche

right (correct) **juste**; (not left) **la droite**
ring (jewellery) **la bague**
ripe **mûr**
river **la rivière**; (big) **le fleuve**
road **la route**; (in town) **la rue**
roasted **rôti**
rock (stone) **le rocher**; (music) **le rock**
roll (bread) **le petit pain**
roof **le toit**
room **la chambre**; (space) **la place**
room service **le room service**
rope **la corde**
rose **la rose**
round (circular) **rond**; it's my round **c'est ma tournée**
roundabout **le rond-point**
row (verb) **ramer**
rowing boat **la barque**
rubber (material) **le caoutchouc**
rubbish **les ordures** (f); **les détritus** (m)
rubbish bin **la poubelle**
rug (mat) **la carpette**; (blanket) **la couverture**
rugby **le rugby**
ruins **les ruines** (f)
ruler **la règle**
rum **le rhum**
run (verb) **courir**
runway **la piste**

S

sad **triste**
safe (not in danger) **en sécurité**; (not dangerous) **sans danger**
safety pin **l'épingle de nourrice** (f)
sailing **la voile**
sailing boat **le voilier**
salad **la salade**
sale **la vente**; (at reduced prices) **les soldes** (f)
salmon **le saumon**
salt **le sel**
same: the same ... **le/la même ...**; the same again, please **la même chose, s'il vous plaît**
sand **le sable**
sandals **les sandales** (f)
sand dunes **les dunes** (f)
sandwich **le sandwich**

sanitary towels **les serviettes hygiéniques** (f)
Saturday **samedi**
sauce **la sauce**
saucer **la soucoupe**
saucepan **la casserole**
sauna **le sauna**
sausage **la saucisse**
say **dire**; what did you say?; **qu'avez-vous dit?**; how do you say ...? **comment dit-on ...?**
scarf **l'écharpe** (f); (head) **le foulard**
schedule **l'emploi du temps** (m)
school **l'école** (f)
science **la science**
scissors **les ciseaux** (m)
Scotland **l'Ecosse** (f)
screen **l'écran** (m)
screw **la vis**
screwdriver **le tournevis**
sea **la mer**
seafood **les fruits de mer** (m)
seat **la place**
seat belt **la ceinture de sécurité**
second (of time) **la seconde**; (in series) **deuxième**
second class **en seconde**
secretary **le/la secrétaire**
see **voir**; I can't see **je ne vois rien**; I see **je vois**
self-employed **à mon compte**
sell **vendre**
seminar **le séminaire**
send **envoyer**
separate **séparé** (adj); (verb) **séparer**
September **septembre**
serious **sérieux**
seven **sept**
seventeen **dix-sept**
seventy **soixante-dix**
several **plusieurs**
sew **coudre**
shampoo **le shampooing**
shave: to shave **se raser**
shaving foam **la mousse à raser**
shawl **le châle**
she **elle**
sheet **le drap**
shell **la coquille**
shellfish **les crustacés** (m)
ship **le bateau**
shirt **la chemise**
shoelaces **les lacets** (m)
shoemaker **la cordonnerie**
shoe polish **le cirage**

shoes **les chaussures** (f)
shop **le magasin**
shopkeeper **commerçant**; (fem) **commerçante**
shopping **les courses** (f); to go shopping **faire les courses**
short **court**; **petit**
shorts **le short**
shoulder **l'épaule** (f)
shower (bath) **la douche**; (rain) **l'averse** (f)
shower gel **le gel douche**
shrimp **la crevette**
shutter (camera) **l'obturateur** (m); (window) **le volet**
sick: I feel sick **j'ai envie de vomir**; to be sick (vomit) **vomir**
side (edge) **le bord**
sidelights **les feux de position** (m)
sightseeing **le tourism**
silk **la soie**
silver (colour) **argenté**; (metal) **l'argent** (m)
simple **simple**
sing **chanter**
single (one) **seul**; (unmarried) **célibataire**
single room **la chambre pour une personne**; **la chambre simple**
single ticket **l'aller simple** (m)
sink **l'évier** (m)
sir **monsieur**
sister **la sœur**
six **six**
sixteen **seize**
sixty **soixante**
size **la taille**
skates **les patins à glace** (m)
ski **le ski**; (verb) **skier**
ski boots **les chaussures de ski** (f)
skid (verb) **déraper**
skiing: to go skiing **faire du ski**
ski lift **le remonte-pente**
skin cleanser **le démaquillant**
ski pole **le bâton de ski**
ski resort **la station de ski**
skirt **la jupe**
sky **le ciel**
sled **la luge**
sleep **le sommeil**; (verb) **dormir**
sleeper **le wagon-lit**
sleeping bag **le sac de couchage**
sleeping pill **le somnifère**

sleeve la manche
slip le jupon
slippers les pantoufles (f)
slow lent
small petit
smell l'odeur (f); (verb) sentir
smile le sourire; (verb) sourire
smoke la fumée; (verb) fumer
snack le snack
snow la neige
so si
soaking solution (for contact lenses) la solution de trempage
soap le savon
socks les chaussettes (f)
soft mou
soft lenses les lentilles souples (f)
soil la terre
somebody quelqu'un
somehow d'une façon ou d'une autre
something quelque chose
sometimes quelquefois
somewhere quelque part
son le fils
song la chanson
sorry (apology) pardon; *sorry?* (pardon?) pardon?; *I'm sorry* je suis désolé
soup la soupe
south le sud
souvenir le souvenir
spade (shovel) la pelle; (garden) la bêche
spades (cards) pique
Spain l'Espagne (f)
Spanish espagnol
spare parts les pièces de rechange (f)
spark plug la bougie
speak parler; *do you speak ...?* parlez-vous ...?; *I don't speak ...* je ne parle pas ...
speed la vitesse
speed limit la limitation de vitesse
spider l'araignée (f)
spinach les épinards (m)
spoon la cuillère
sport le sport
sports centre le centre sportif
spring (mechanical) le ressort; (season) le printemps
square (in town) la place; (adj: shape) carré

stadium le stade
staircase l'escalier (m)
stairs les escaliers (m)
stamp le timbre
stapler l'agrafeuse (f)
star l'étoile (f); (movie) la vedette
start (beginning) le début; (verb) commencer
starters les entrées (f)
statement la déposition
station la gare; (underground) la station
statue la statue
steak le steak
steal voler; *it's been stolen* on l'a volé
steamed à la vapeur
steamer le bateau à vapeur; (cooking) le couscoussier
steering wheel le volant
sting la piqûre; (verb) piquer
stockings les bas (m)
stomach l'estomac (m)
stomach ache le mal de ventre, le mal à l'estomac
stop (bus) l'arrêt (de bus) (m); (verb) s'arrêter
storm la tempête
straight on tout droit
strawberry la fraise
stream (small river) le ruisseau
street la rue
street musician le musicien des rues
string (cord) la ficelle; (guitar etc) la corde
strong (person, drink) fort; (material) résistant
student l'étudiant (m)
stupid stupide
suburbs la banlieue
sugar le sucre
suit le costume; *it suits you* ça vous va bien
suitcase la valise
summer l'été (m)
sun le soleil
sunbathe se faire bronzer
sunburn le coup de soleil
Sunday dimanche
sunglasses les lunettes de soleil (f)
sunny ensoleillé
sunshade le parasol
suntan le bronzage
suntan lotion la lotion solaire
supermarket le supermarché
supper le souper

supplement le supplément
suppository le suppositoire
sure sûr
surname le nom de famille
sweat la transpiration; (verb) transpirer
sweater le pull
sweatshirt le sweat-shirt
sweet (not sour) sucré; (confectionery) le bonbon
swim (verb) nager
swimming la natation; *to go swimming* aller se baigner
swimming pool la piscine
swimming trunks le maillot de bain
swimsuit le maillot de bain
Swiss suisse(sse)
switch l'interrupteur (m)
Switzerland la Suisse
synagogue la synagogue
syringe la seringue
syrup le sirop

T

table la table
tablet le cachet
take prendre
take away: to take away à emporter
takeoff le décollage
talcum powder le talc
talk la conversation; (verb) parler
tall grand
tampon le tampon
tangerine la mandarine
tap (water) le robinet
tapestry la tapisserie
taxi le taxi
tea le thé
teacher (secondary) le professeur
telephone le téléphone; (verb) téléphoner
telephone box la cabine téléphonique
television la télévision
temperature la température
ten dix
tennis le tennis
tent la tente
tent peg le piquet de tente
tent pole le montant de tente
terminal le terminal
terrace la terrasse
than que
thank (verb) remercier; *thank you* merci; *thanks* merci

that (that one) **ça**; *that bus* **ce bus**; *that man* **cet homme**; *that woman* **cette femme**; *what's that?* **qu'est-ce que c'est?**; *I think that the ...* **je pense que le ...**

the **le/la**; (plural) **les**

theatre **le théâtre**

their: *their room* **leur chambre**; *their books* **leurs livres**; *it's theirs* **c'est à eux**

them: *it's them* **ce sont eux/elles**; *it's for them* **c'est pour eux/elles**; *give it to them* **donnez-le-leur**

then **alors**; (after) **ensuite**

there **là**; *there is/are ...* **il y a ...**

these: *these things* **ces choses**; *these are mine* **ils sont à moi**

they **ils**; (fem) **elles**

thick **épais**

thief **le voleur**

thin **mince, maigre**

think **penser**; *I think so* **je pense que oui**; *I'll think about it* **je vais y penser**

third **troisième**

thirsty: *I'm thirsty* **j'ai soif**

thirteen **treize**

thirty **trente**

this (this one) **ceci**; *this bus* **ce bus**; *this man* **cet homme**; *this woman* **cette femme**; *what's this?* **qu'est-ce que c'est?**; *this is Mr ...* **je vous présente M. ...**

those: *those things* **ces choses-là**; *those are his* **ils sont à lui**

three **trois**

throat **la gorge**

throat pastilles **les pastilles pour la gorge** (f)

through **à travers**

thunderstorm **l'orage** (m)

Thursday **jeudi**

ticket **le billet**; (underground, bus) **le ticket**

ticket collector **le contrôleur**

ticket office **le guichet**

tide **la marée**

tie **la cravate**; (verb) **nouer**

tight **étroit**

tights **les collants** (m)

tiles, tiling **le carrelage**

time **l'heure** (f); *what's the time?* **quelle heure est-il?**

timetable (train, bus) **l'horaire** (f)

tip (money) **le pourboire**; (end) **le bout**

tired **fatigué**

tissues **mouchoirs**

to: *to England* **en Angleterre**; *to Paris* **à Paris**; *to the station* **à la gare**; *to the centre* **au centre**; *to the doctor* **chez le docteur**

toast **le pain grillé**

tobacco **le tabac**

toboggan **le toboggan**

today **aujourd'hui**

together **ensemble**

toilet paper **le papier hygiénique**

toilets **les toilettes** (f)

tomato **la tomate**

tomorrow **demain**; *see you tomorrow* **à demain**

tongue **la langue**

tonic **le tonic**

tonight **ce soir**

too (also) **aussi**; (excessively) **trop**

tooth **la dent**

toothache **le mal de dents**

toothbrush **la brosse à dents**

toothpaste **le dentifrice**

torch **la lampe de poche**

tour **la visite**

tourist **le/la touriste**

tourist office **le syndicat d'initiative**

towel **la serviette**

tower **la tour**

town **la ville**

town centre **le centre-ville**

town hall **l'hôtel de ville** (m); **la mairie**

toy **le jouet**

track suit **le survêtement**

tractor **le tracteur**

trade fair **la foire-exposition**

tradition **la tradition**

traffic **la circulation, le trafic**

traffic lights **les feux** (m)

trailer **la remorque**

train **le train**

trainee **le stagiaire**

trainers **les tennis** (m)

translate **traduire**

translator **le traducteur**

travel agency **l'agence de voyages** (f)

traveller's cheque **le chèque de voyage**

tray **le plateau**

tree **l'arbre** (m)

trolley **le chariot**

trousers **le pantalon**

truck **le camion**

true **vrai**

try **essayer**

Tuesday **mardi**

tunnel **le tunnel**

tweezers **la pince à épiler**

twelve **douze**

twenty **vingt**

two **deux**

tyre **le pneu**

U

ugly **laid**

umbrella **le parapluie**

uncle **l'oncle** (m)

under ... **sous ...**

underground **le métro**

underpants **le slip**

understand **comprendre**; *I understand* **je comprends**; *I don't understand* **je ne comprends pas**

underwear **les sous-vêtements** (f)

university **l'université** (f)

university lecturer **le maître de conférences**

unleaded **sans plomb**

until **jusqu'à**

unusual **inhabituel**

up **en haut**; (upward) **vers le haut**; *up there* **là-haut**

urgent **urgent**

us: *it's us* **c'est nous**; *it's for us* **c'est pour nous**; *give it to us* **donnez-le-nous**

use (verb) **utiliser**; *it's no use* **ça ne sert à rien**

useful **utile**

usual **habituel**

usually **d'habitude**

V

vacancy (room) **la chambre à louer**

vaccination **la vaccination**

vacuum cleaner **l'aspirateur** (m)

valley **la vallée**

valve **la soupape**

vanilla **la vanille**

vase **le vase**

VCR **le magnètoscope**

veal **le veau**

vegetables **les légumes** (m)

vegetarian (adj) **végétarien**

vehicle le véhicule
very très; *very much* beaucoup
vet le vétérinaire
video (film/tape) la vidéo
view la vue
viewfinder le viseur
villa la villa
village le village
vinegar le vinaigre
violin le violon
visit la visite; (verb: place) visiter; (person) rendre visite
visitor le visiteur
vitamin pill le comprimé de vitamines
vodka la vodka
voice la voix
voicemail la messagerie téléphonique

W

wait attendre; *wait!* attendez!
waiter le serveur; *waiter!* garçon!
waiting room la salle d'attente
waitress la serveuse; *waitress!* Mademoiselle!
Wales le pays de Galles
walk (verb) marcher; *to go for a walk* aller se promener
wall (inside) la paroi; (outside) le mur
wallet le portefeuille
want (verb) vouloir; *I would like* je voudrais
war la guerre
wardrobe l'armoire (f)
warm chaud
was: I was j'étais; *he was* il était; *she was* elle était; *it was* il/elle était
washer la rondelle
washing machine la machine à laver
washing powder la lessive
washing-up liquid le produit pour la vaisselle

wasp la guêpe
watch la montre; (verb) regarder
water l'eau (f)
waterfall la chute d'eau
water heater le chauffe-eau
wave la vague; (verb) faire signe de la main
wavy (hair) ondulé
we nous
weather le temps
Web site le site web
wedding le mariage
Wednesday mercredi
weeds les mauvais herbes (f)
week la semaine
welcome: you're welcome je vous en prie
Wellington boots les boîtes en caoutchouc (f)
were: we were nous étions; *you were* vous étiez; *they were* ils/elles étaient
west l'ouest
wet mouillé
what? comment?; *what is it?* qu'est-ce que c'est?
wheel la roue
wheelchair le fauteuil roulant; la chaise roulante
when? quand?
where? où?
whether si
which? lequel?
whisky le whisky
white blanc, (fem) blanche
who? qui?
why? pourquoi?
wide large
wife la femme
wind le vent
window la fenêtre
windscreen le pare-brise
wine le vin
wine list la carte des vins
wine merchant le négociant en vins
wing l'aile (f)
winter l'hiver (m)
with avec; *with pleasure* avec plaisir

withdraw (verb) retirer
without sans
witness le témoin
woman la femme
wood le bois
wool la laine
word le mot
work le travail; (verb) travailler; (machine etc) fonctionner
worktop le plan de travail
worse pire
worst le pire
wrapping paper le papier d'emballage; (for presents) le papier cadeau
wrench la clé anglaise
wrist le poignet
write (verb) écrire; *written by* écrit par
writing paper le papier à lettres
wrong faux, (fem) fausse

X, Y, Z

x-ray radio
x-ray departement la salle de radiology
year l'an (m); l'année (f)
yellow jaune
yes oui
yesterday hier
yet déjà; *not yet* pas encore
yoghurt le yaourt
you (singular informal) tu; (plural; singular formal) vous
young jeune
your (singular informal): *your book* ton livre; *your house* ta maison; *your shoes* tes chaussures; *it's yours* c'est à toi; (plural; singular formal): *your house* votre maison; *your shoes* vos chaussures; *it's yours* c'est à vous
youth hostel l'auberge de jeunesse (f)
zip la fermeture éclair
zoo le zoo

DICTIONARY
French to English

The gender of French nouns listed here is indicated by the abbreviations (m) and (f), for masculine and feminine. Plural nouns are indicated by (m pl) or (f pl). French adjectives (adj) vary according to the gender and number of the word they describe; the masculine form is shown here. In most cases, you add an **-e** to the masculine form to make it feminine. Certain endings use a different rule: masculine adjectives that end in **-x** adopt an **-se** ending in the feminine form, while those that end in **-ien** change to **-ienne**. Some feminine adjectives that do not follow these rules are shown here and follow the abbreviation (fem). For the plural form, a (silent) **-s** is usually added.

A

à: *at:* **à la poste** *at the post office;* **à trois heures** *at 3 o'clock;* **à côté de** *beside;* **à demain** *see you tomorrow;* **à emporter** *to take away;* **à travers** *through*
abat-jour (m) *lampshade*
abricot (m) *apricot*
accélérateur (m) *accelerator*
accident (m) *accident*
acheter *to buy*
adaptateur (m) *adaptor* (voltage)
addition (f) *bill*
adhésif (m) *adhesive*
adresse (f) *address*
adresse électronique (f) *email address*
aéroglisseur (m) *hovercraft*
aéroport (m) *airport*
affaire (f) *bargain*
affaires (f pl) *business*
affiche (f) *poster* (outside)
affreux *awful*
agence de voyages (f) *travel agency*
agenda (m) *diary*
agent (m) *agent*
agneau (m) *lamb*
agrafeuse (f) *stapler*
agrandissement (m) *enlargement*
aide (f) *help*
aider *to help*
aiguille (f) *needle;* **aiguille à tricoter** *knitting needle*
ail (m) *garlic*
aile (f) *wing*
ailleurs *somewhere else*

aimer *to like/love;* **j'aime nager** *I like swimming;* **je n'aime pas** *I don't like*
air (m) *air*
alcool (m) *alcohol*
Algérie (f) *Algeria*
algérien(ne) *Algerian*
allée (f) *path*
Allemagne (f) *Germany*
allemand(e) *German*
aller *to go*
aller chercher *to get* (fetch)
allergique *allergic*
aller patiner *to go ice-skating*
aller retour (m) *return ticket*
aller simple (m) *single ticket*
allez-vous en! *go away!*
allumage (m) *ignition*
allumette (f) *match* (light)
alors *well then*
Alpes: les Alpes (m pl) *Alps*
amant (m) *lover*
ambassade (f) *embassy*
ambulance (f) *ambulance*
amer *bitter*
américain(e) *American*
Amérique (f) *America*
ami(e) *friend*
amical *friendly*
amour (m) *love*
amphithéâtre (m) *lecture theatre*
ampoule (f) *blister; light bulb*
an (m) *year*
ananas (m) *pineapple*
Andorre *Andorra*
anglais(e) *English*

Angleterre (f) *England*
animaux (familiers) (m pl) *pets*
animé *busy* (street)
année (f) *year*
anniversaire (m) *birthday*
annuaire (m) *directory* (telephone)
antigel (m) *antifreeze*
antiseptique (m) *antiseptic*
août *August*
apéritif (m) *aperitif*
appareil acoustique (m) *hearing aid*
appareil-photo (m) *camera*
appartement (m) *apartment*
appât (m) *bait*
appétit (m) *appetite*
apprendre *to learn*
après *after*
après-midi (m) *afternoon*
après-rasage (m) *aftershave*
araignée (f) *spider*
arbre (m) *tree*
arbre à cames (m) *camshaft*
architecture (f) *architecture*
arête (f) *fishbone*
argent (m) *cash; money; silver* (metal)
argenté *silver* (colour)
armoire (f) *wardrobe*
arrêt de bus (m) *bus stop*
arrière (m) *back* (not front)
arrivée (f) *arrival*
arriver *to arrive*
art (m) *art*
artiste (m) *artist*
ascenseur (m) *lift*

aspirateur (m) *vacuum cleaner*

aspirine (f) *aspirin*

assez *enough; fairly*

assiette (f) *plate*

assurance (f) *insurance*

asthmatique *asthmatic*

attaché-case (m) *briefcase*

attendez! *wait!*

attendre *to wait*

attention! *careful!*

atterrir *to land*

attirant *attractive*

au: au café *at the café;* au revoir *goodbye*

auberge (f) *inn*

auberge de jeunesse (f) *youth hostel*

aucun *not any; none*

au-dessus de *over (above)*

aujourd'hui *today*

aussi *too (also)*

Australie (f) *Australia*

australien(ne) *Australian*

automatique *automatic*

automne (m) *autumn*

autoroute (f) *motorway*

autre: autre chose *something else*

avance (f) *advance*

avant *before*

avec *with;* avec plasir *with pleasure*

averse (f) *shower (rain)*

aveugle *blind (cannot see)*

avion (m) *aircraft*

avocat (m) *avocado*

avocat(e) *lawyer*

avoir *to have*

avril *April*

B

bac (m) *ferry (small)*

bagages (m pl) *luggage; baggage;* bagages à main (m pl) *hand luggage*

baigner: aller se baigner *to go swimming*

bain (m) *bath*

balai (m) *broom*

balcon (m) *balcony*

balle (f) *ball (tennis etc)*

ballon (m) *ball (football etc)*

banane (f) *banana*

bandage (m) *bandage*

banlieue (f) *suburbs*

banque (f) *bank*

bar (m) *bar (place)*

barbe (f) *beard*

barbecue (m) *barbecue*

barque (f) *rowing boat*

bas (m) *stockings;* low (adj); en bas *down*

bateau (m) *boat; ship;* bateau à moteur (m) *motorboat;* bateau à vapeur (m) *steamer*

bâtiment (m) *building*

bâton de ski (m) *ski pole*

batterie (f) *battery (car)*

baume après-shampooing (m) *conditioner (hair)*

beau, (fem) belle *beautiful*

bébé (m) *baby*

bêche (f) *spade (garden)*

beige *beige*

beignet (m) *doughnut*

belge *Belgian*

Belgique: la Belgique *Belgium*

bénéfices (m pl) *profits*

béquilles (f pl) *crutches*

besoin: avoir besoin de *to need;* j'ai besoin de ... *I need ...*

beurre (m) *butter*

bibliothèque (f) *library*

bicyclette (f) *bicycle*

bien sûr *of course*

bien! *good!;* ça vous va bien *it suits you*

bière (f) *beer*

bijouterie (f) *jeweller's*

billet (m) *ticket; banknote*

biscuit (m) *biscuit*

blanc, (fem) blanche *white*

blanchisserie (f) *laundry (place)*

blême *pale*

blessure (f) *injury*

bleu (m) *bruise;* blue (adj)

bloc notes (m) *notepad*

blond (adj) *blond*

bœuf (m) *beef*

boire *to drink;* vous voulez boire quelque chose? *would you like something to drink?*

bois (m) *wood*

boisson (f) *drink*

boîte (f) *box;* boîte à lettres *postbox;* boîte de chocolats *box of chocolates;* boîte de conserve *can (vessel);* boîte de nuit *nightclub;* boîte de vitesses *gearbox*

boîtes en caoutchouc (f pl) *Wellington boots*

bol (m) *bowl*

bon, (fem) bonne *good*

bonbon (m) *sweet (confectionery);* bonbons à la menthe (m pl) *peppermints*

bondé *crowded*

bonjour *hello*

bon marché *inexpensive; cheap*

bonne chance! *good luck!*

bonsoir *good evening*

bord (m) *side (edge)*

botte (f) *boot (footwear)*

bouche (f) *mouth*

boucherie (f) *butcher's*

bouchon (m) *plug (sink); cork*

boucles (f pl) *curls*

boucles d'oreille (f pl) *earrings*

bouger *to move;* ne bougez pas! *don't move!*

bougie (f) *spark plug; candle*

bouilli *boiled*

bouillir *to boil*

bouilloire (f) *kettle*

boulangerie (f) *bakery*

bout (m) *tip, end*

bouteille (f) *bottle*

bouton (m) *button;* boutons de manchette (m pl) *cuff links*

bracelet (m) *bracelet*

branche (f) *branch*

bras (m) *arm*

Bretagne: la Bretagne *Brittany*

bretelles (f pl) *braces (clothes)*

briquet (m) *lighter*

britannique *British*

broche (f) *brooch*

brochure (f) *brochure*

broderie (f) *embroidery*

bronzage (m) *suntan*

bronzer: se faire bronzer *to sunbathe*

brosse (f) *brush;* brosse à dents (f) *toothbrush*

brosser *to brush*

brouillard (m) *fog*

brûler *to burn*

brûlure (f) *burn*
Bruxelles *Brussels*
bruyant *noisy*
budget (m) *budget*
bunker (m) *bunker*
bureau (m) *desk; office*
bureau de location (m) *box office*
bus (m) *bus*

C

ça *that (that one)*
cabine téléphonique (f) *telephone box*
cacahuètes (f pl) *peanuts*
cachet (m) *tablet*
cadeau (m) *gift*
cadenas (m) *padlock*
cadre (m) *executive (in company)*
cafard (m) *cockroach*
café (m) *café; coffee*; **café crème** *white coffee*; **café soluble** *instant coffee*
cage (f) *cage*
caisse (f) *check-out (supermarket)*
calculette (f) *calculator*
cambriolage (m) *burglary*
caméscope (m) *camcorder*
camion (m) *truck*
campagne (f) *countryside*
camping-car (m) *camper van*
Canada (m) *Canada*
canadien(ne) *Canadian*
canal (m) *canal*
canif (m) *penknife*
canne à pêche (f) *fishing rod*
canoë (m) *canoe*
caoutchouc (m) *rubber (material)*
capot (m) *car bonnet*
capsule (f) *cap (bottle)*
caravane (f) *caravan*
carburateur (m) *carburettor*
carnet (m) *notebook*; **carnet de chèques** (m) *chequebook*
carotte (f) *carrot*
carpette (f) *rug (mat)*
carré *square (adj: shape)*
carreau *diamonds (cards)*

carrelage (m) *tiles, tiling*
carte (f) *menu; card; map*; **carte bancaire** *debit card*; **carte de crédit** *credit card*; **carte d'embarquement** *boarding pass*; **carte des vins** *wine list*; **carte de visite** *business card*; **carte postale** *postcard*; **carte téléphonique** *phonecard*
casquette (f) *cap (hat)*
cassé *broken*
casserole (f) *saucepan*
cassette (f) *cassette*
cassis (m) *blackcurrant*
cathédrale (f) *cathedral*
cave (f) *cellar*
ce (bus) *that (bus)*
ceci *this (this one)*
ceinture (f) *belt*; **ceinture de sécurité** *seat belt*
célibataire *single (unmarried)*
cellule photoélectrique (f) *light meter*
cendrier (m) *ashtray*
cent *hundred*
centre (m) *centre*; **centre sportif** *sports centre*
centre-ville (m) *town centre*
cerise (f) *cherry*
certificat (m) *certificate*
ces (choses) *these (things)*
c'est *it's*; **c'est tout** *that's all*
cet (homme) *that (man)*
cette (femme) *that (woman)*
chaise (f) *chair*
châle (m) *shawl*
chambre (f) *bedroom*; **chambre à louer** *vacancy*; **chambre pour deux personnes** *double room*; **chambre simple** *single room*
chambre à air (f) *inner tube*
champ (m) *field (farming)*
champignon (m) *mushroom*
chance (f) *luck*
changer *to change (money)*; **se changer** *to change (clothes)*
chanson (f) *song*
chanter *to sing*
chapeau (m) *hat*
chaque *each; every*
charcuterie (f) *delicatessen*

chargeur (m) *charger*
chariot (m) *trolley*
charpentier (m) *carpenter*
chat (m) *cat*
château (m) *castle*
chaud *hot; warm*; **j'ai chaud** *I feel hot*
chauffage (m) *heating*; **chauffage central** *central heating*
chauffe-eau (m) *boiler; water heater*
chaussettes (f pl) *socks*
chaussures (f pl) *shoes*; **chaussures de ski** (f pl) *ski boots*
chauve *bald*
chef (m) *manager*; **chef d'orchestre** *conductor (orchestra)*; **chef de train** *guard (train)*
chemin (m) *path*
chemin de fer (m) *railway*
cheminée (f) *fireplace; chimney*
chemise (f) *shirt*; **chemise de nuit** *nightdress*
chemisier (m) *blouse*
chèque (m) *cheque*; **chèque de voyage** *traveller's cheque*
cher *expensive*; **pas cher** *inexpensive*
cheveux (m pl) *hair*; **les cheveux longs/courts** *long/short hair*
cheville (f) *ankle*
chez *at home*; **chez moi** *at my house*; **chez vous** *at your place*
chien (m) *dog*
chiffon à poussière (m) *duster*
chiffres (m pl) *figures*
chips (f pl) *crisps*
chocolat (m) *chocolate*
chou (m) *cabbage*
chou-fleur (m) *cauliflower*
chute d'eau (f) *waterfall*
ciel (m) *sky*
cigare (m) *cigar*
cigarette (f) *cigarette*
cimetière (m) *cemetery*
cinéma (m) *cinema*
cinq *five*
cinquante *fifty*
cintre (m) *coat hanger*
cirage (m) *shoe polish*
circulation (f) *traffic*
ciseaux (m pl) *scissors*

citron (m) *lemon*; **citron vert** *lime*
clair *clear; light (not dark)*
classe (f) *class*
clavier (m) *keyboard*
clé (f) *key*; **clé anglaise** (f) *wrench*
clignotant (m) *indicator*
climatisation (f) *air conditioning*
cloche (f) *bell (church)*
clou (m) *nail (metal)*
cocktail (m) *cocktail party*
code (m) *PIN*
code de la route (m) *highway code*
code postal (m) *postcode*
cœur (m) *heart*; **problème au cœur** *heart condition*;
cœurs (m pl) *hearts (cards)*
coffre (m) *boot (car)*
cognac (m) *brandy*
coiffeur (m) *hairdresser; barber's*
coin (m) *corner*
col (m) *collar*
colis (m) *parcel*
collants (m pl) *tights*
colle (f) *glue*
collection (f) *collection (stamps etc)*
collier (m) *collar; necklace*
colline (f) *hill*
combien? *how much?*;
combien ça coûte? *how much does it cost?*
comme *like (similar to)*
commencer *to start*
comment? *how?*; **comment allez-vous?** *how are you?*;
comment est-ce que ça s'appelle? *what's it called?*; **comment vous appelez-vous?** *what's your name?*
commerçant(e) *shopkeeper*
commissariat (m) *police station*
commode (f) *chest of drawers*
compagnie (f) *company*; **compagnie aérienne** *airline*
compartiment (m) *compartment*
complet *full*
compliqué *complicated*
comprendre *to understand*; **je comprends** *I*

understand; **je ne comprends pas** *I don't understand*
comprimé (m) *pill*; **comprimé de vitamines** *vitamin pill*
comptable (m/f) *accountant*
compte: à mon compte *self-employed*
concert (m) *concert*
concierge (m/f) *caretaker*
concombre (m) *cucumber*
conducteur (m) *driver*
conduire *to drive*
conférence (f) *conference*
confiseur (m) *confectioner*
confiture (f) *jam*
congélateur (m) *freezer*
connaître *to know (person)*
consigne automatique (f) *luggage lockers*
constructeur (m) *builder*
consulat (m) *consulate*
consultant(e) *consultant*
contraceptif (m) *contraceptive*
contre *against*
contrôle des passeports (m) *passport control*
contrôleur (m) *ticket collector*
conversation (f) *talk*
copieur (m) *photocopier*
coquille (f) *shell*
corde (f) *rope; string (guitar etc)*
cordonnerie (f) *shoemaker*
corne (f) *horn (animal)*
corps (m) *body*
correspondant (m) *pen pal*
corse *Corsican*
Corse: la Corse *Corsica*
costume (m) *suit*
côtelette (f) *chop (food)*
coton (m) *cotton*; **coton hydrophile** *cotton balls*
cou (m) *neck*
couche (f) *nappy*; **couches à jeter** (f pl) *disposable nappies*
coude (m) *elbow*
coudre *to sew*
couette (f) *duvet*
couleur (f) *colour*
couloir (m) *corridor*
coup de soleil (m) *sunburn*

coupe (de cheveux) (f) *haircut*
couper *to cut, chop*
coupure (f) *cut*
courant (m) *current*
courgette (f) *courgette*
courir *to run*
courroie du ventilateur (f) *fan belt*
courses (f pl) *shopping*; **to go shopping faire les courses**
court *short*
couscoussier (m) *steamer (cooking)*
cousin (m) *cousin*
couteau (m) *knife*
coûter *to cost*
couverture (f) *blanket; rug*
crabe (m) *crab*
crampe (f) *cramp*
cravate (f) *tie*
crayon (m) *pencil*
crème (f) *cream*; **crème anti-insecte** (f) *insect repellent cream*
crêpe (f) *pancake*
crevaison (f) *puncture*
crevette (f) *shrimp*
crier *to cry (shout)*
croisière (f) *cruise*
crustacés (m) *shellfish*
cuillère (f) *spoon*
cuir (m) *leather*
cuire *to bake*
cuisine (f) *kitchen*
cuisinier (m) *cook*
cuisinière (f) *cooker*
curry (m) *curry*

D

d'accord *OK*
danger *danger*; **sans danger** *safe*
dans *in*
danse (f) *dance*
danser *to dance*
de *of*
début (m) *start (beginning)*
débutant(e) *beginner*
décapsuleur (m) *bottle opener*
décembre *December*
décollage (m) *takeoff*
décolorer *to bleach*
décorateur (m) *decorator*
dehors *outside*
déjà *yet; already*
déjeuner (m) *lunch*

delco (m) *distributor* (car)
demain *tomorrow*
démaquillant (m)
  skin cleanser
déménager *to move house*
demi *half*; **une demi-heure**
  half an hour
demi-pension (f) *half*
  board
dent (f) *tooth*
dentelle (f) *lace*
dentier (m) *dentures*
dentifrice (m) *toothpaste*
dentiste (m/f) *dentist*
déodorant (m) *deodorant*
départ (m) *departures*
département (f)
  department
dépliant (m) *leaflet*
déposition (f) *statement*
déraper *skid* (verb)
dernier *last* (final); **la**
  semaine dernière *last*
  week
derrière *behind*
descendre *to get off*
  (bus etc)
designer (m) *designer*
désolé: je suis désolé(e)
  I'm sorry
desserts (m pl) *desserts*
détritus (m) *rubbish*
deux *two*; **les deux** *both*
deuxième *second*
  (in series)
devant *in front of*
développer *to develop*
d'habitude *usually*
diabétique *diabetic*
diamant (m) *diamond*
  (jewel)
diarrhée (f) *diarrhoea*
dictionnaire (m) *dictionary*
diesel (m) *diesel*
différent *different*;
  c'est différent *that's*
  different
difficile *difficult*
dimanche *Sunday*
dîner (m) *dinner*
dire *to say*; **qu'avez-vous**
  dit? *what did you say?*;
  comment dit-on ...?
  how do you say ...?;
  qu'est-ce que cela veut
  dire? *what does this*
  mean?
directeur (m) *director*
discothèque (m) *disco*
disquaire (m) *record*
  shop

disque (m) *record* (music);
  disque compact (m)
  compact disc
distributeur automatique
  (m) *cash machine*
divertissement (m)
  entertainment
divorcé *divorced*
dix *ten*
dix-huit *eighteen*
dix-neuf *nineteen*
dix-sept *seventeen*
docteur (m) *doctor*
document (m) *document*
doigt (m) *finger*
dois: je dois ... *I must ...*
dollar (m) *dollar*
donner *give*
dormir *to sleep*
dos (m) *back* (body)
douane (f) *customs*
doubler *to overtake*
  (in a car)
douche (f) *shower*
  (bath)
douleur (f) *ache*; *pain*
douze *twelve*
drap (m) *sheet*
drapeau (m) *flag*
draps (m pl) *bed linen*
droit (m) *law*
droite *right* (not left)
drôle *funny*
dunes (f pl) *sand dunes*
dur *hard*

E

eau (f) *water*; **eau gazeuse**
  fizzy water; **eau minérale**
  mineral water; **eau potable**
  drinking water; **eau de**
  Javel *bleach*
échanger *to exchange*
écharpe (f) *scarf*
échecs (m pl) *chess*
école (f) *school*
Ecosse: l'Ecosse (f)
  Scotland
écouteurs (m) *headphones*
écran (m) *screen*
écrevisse (f) *crayfish*
  (freshwater)
écrire *to write*; **écrit**
  par ... *written by ...*
écrou (m) *nut* (for bolt)
église (f) *church*
élastique (m) *elastic band*;
  elastic (adj)
électricien(ne) *electrician*
électricité (f) *electricity*

électrique *electric*
elle *she*
elles *they* (fem)
email (m) *email*
embrayage (m) *clutch*
émeraude (f) *emerald*
emplacement (m) *pitch*
emploi du temps (m)
  schedule
en *in*; **en France** *in France*
enchanté(e) *pleased to meet*
  you
encore: encore un café
  another coffee
encre (f) *ink*
endormi *asleep*
endroit (m) *place*
enfant (m) *child*
enfin! *at last!*
ennuyeux *boring*
enregistrement (m) *check-in*;
  enregistrement des
  bagages *baggage*
  check-in
ensemble *together*
ensoleillé *sunny*
ensuite *then* (after)
entendre *hear*
entre ... between ...
entrée (f) *entrance*
entrées (f pl) *starters*
enveloppe (f) *envelope*
envie: j'ai envie de ...
  I feel like ...
environ *about*
envoyer *to send*
épais *thick*
épaule (f) *shoulder*
épicerie (f) *grocer's*
épileptique *epileptic*
épinards (m) *spinach*
épingle (f) *pin*;
  épingle de nourrice
  safety pin
erreur (f) *mistake*
escalier (m) *stairs*; *staircase*;
  escalier roulant
  escalator
Espagne: l'Espagne (f)
  Spain
espagnol *Spanish*
essayer *to try*
essence (f) *petrol*
essieu (m) *axle*
est (m) *east*
est *is*; **il/elle est** *he/she is*;
  c'est *it is*
estimation (f) *estimate*
estomac (m) *stomach*
et *and*
étage (m) *floor* (storey)

été (m) summer
étiquette (f) label
étoile (f) star
étouffant close (stuffy)
étranger (m) foreigner
étroit narrow; tight
étudiant (m) student
eux: c'est à eux it's theirs;
   c'est pour eux/elles it's
   for them
évanouir to faint
évier (m) sink
excédent de bagages (m)
   excess baggage
excellent excellent
excursion (f) excursion
exemple (m) example
exposition (f) exhibition
exprès deliberately
extérieure (m) exterior;
   exterior (adj)
   exterior **extincteur** (m)
   fire extinguisher

F

face: en face de opposite
facile easy
façon: d'une façon ou
   d'une autre somehow
facteur (m) postman
facture (f) invoice
faim: j'ai faim I'm hungry
faire to do; make;
   faire de autostop
   to hitchhike; **faire**
   du jogging to jog;
   faire enregistrer ses
   bagages to check in;
   faire la cuisine to
   cook; **faire la queue**
   to queue (verb);
   faire signe de la main
   to wave
fan (m/f) fan (enthusiast)
fantastique fantastic
farine (f) flour
fatigué tired
fauteuil (m) armchair;
   fauteuil roulant (m)
   wheelchair
faux, (fem) **fausse** wrong
fax (m) fax; fax machine
félicitations! congratulations!
femme (f) woman;
   wife; **femme de chambre**
   maid; **femme de**
   ménages cleaner
fenêtre (f) window
fer à repasser (m) iron
   (for clothes)

ferme (f) farm
fermé closed
fermer to close
fermeture éclair (f) zip
fermier (m) farmer
ferry (m) ferry (large)
fête (f) party (celebration)
feu (m) fire; **feu d'artifice**
   fireworks; **feu de camp**
   campfire
feuille (f) leaf
feutre (m) felt-tip pen
feux (m pl) lights; traffic lights;
   feux de position (m pl)
   sidelights
fevrier February
fiancé engaged (couple)
fiancé(e) fiancé(e)
ficelle (f) string (cord)
fièvre (f) fever
figue (f) fig
fille (f) girl; daughter
film (m) film
fils (m) son
fin (f) end
fini over (finished)
flash (m) flash (camera)
fleur (f) flower
fleuriste (f) florist
fleuve (m) river (big)
flûte (f) flute
foie (m) liver
foire (f) fair;
   foire-exposition trade
   fair
foncé dark; **bleu foncé**
   dark blue
fonctionner function
   (machine, etc)
fond (m) bottom
football (m) football
forêt (f) forest
formulaire de demande
   (m) application form
fort loud; strong (person,
   drink)
fou, (fem) **folle** mad
foulard (m) headscarf
four (m) oven
fourchette (f) fork
frais, (fem) **fraîche** cool
fraise (f) strawberry
framboise (f) raspberry
français(e) French
France: la France France
frange (f) fringe
frein (m) brake; **frein à main**
   handbrake
freiner to brake
frère (m) brother
frigo (m) fridge

frire to fry
frit fried
frites (f pl) chips
froid (adj) cold
fromage (m) cheese
fromagerie (f) cheese shop
frontière (f) border
fruit (m) fruit
fruits de mer (m pl)
   seafood
fumée (f) smoke
fumer to smoke
fusil (m) rifle

G

galerie d'art (f) art gallery
gamelle (f) animal's bowl
gants (m pl) gloves
garage (m) garage
garagiste (m) mechanic
garantie (f) guarantee
garantir to guarantee
garçon (m) boy;
   garçon! waiter!
gare (f) station; **gare**
   routière (f) bus station
garer to park
garniture (f) filling
   (in sandwich, cake)
gâteau (m) cake
gauche left (not right)
gaz (m) gas; **gaz à briquet**
   (m) lighter fluid
gazoile (m) diesel
gel (m) gel; frost; **gel douche**
   (m) shower gel
gênant embarrassing
genou (m) knee
gens (m pl) people
gentil friendly; kind
gilet (m) cardigan
gin (m) gin
gingembre (m) ginger
glace (f) ice; ice cream
golf (m) golf
gomme (f) eraser
gorge (f) throat
goût (m) flavour
goutes (f pl) drops
gouttière (f) gutter
gouvernement (m)
   government
grand big; large; tall; **grand**
   magasin (m) department
   store
Grande-Bretagne (f)
   Great Britain
grand-mère (f)
   grandmother
grand-père (m) grandfather

grands-parents (m pl) *grandparents*
gras (m) *fat (on meat, etc)*
gratuit *free (of charge)*
grenier (m) *attic*
gril (m) *grill*
grillé(e) *grilled*
gris *grey*
gros, (fem) grosse (adj) *fat*
grotte (f) *cave*
groupe (m) *group; band (musicians)*
guêpe (f) *wasp*
guerre (f) *war*
gueule de bois (f) *hangover*
guichet (m) *cashier; ticket office*
guide (m) *guide; guide book;* **guide de conversation** (m) *phrase book*
guitare (f) *guitar*

H

habituel *ordinary; usual*
hache (f) *axe*
haie (f) *hedge*
hamburger (m) *hamburger*
hamster (m) *hamster*
handicapé *disabled*
haricots (m pl) *beans*
haut *high;* **en haut** *up;* **vers la haut** *upwards;* **là-haut** *up there*
hébergement (m) *accommodation*
hépatite (f) *hepatitis*
herbe (f) *grass*
heure (f) *hour; time*
heures d'ouverture (f pl) *opening times*
heureux *glad; happy*
hier *yesterday*
histoire (f) *history*
hiver (m) *winter*
homard (m) *lobster*
homéopathie *homeopathy*
homme (m) *man*
homosexuel *gay*
honnête *honest*
hôpital (m) *hospital*
horaire (f) *timetable (train, bus)*
horloge (f) *clock*
horrible *horrible*
hors-taxe *duty-free*
hôte (m) *host*
hôtel (m) *hotel*
hôtel de ville (m) *town hall*

hôtesse(f) *hostess;* **hôtesse de air** *flight attendant*
hoverport (m) *hoverport*
huile (f) *oil*
huit *eight*
huître (f) *oyster*
hydrofoil (m) *hydrofoil*

I

identification (f) *identification*
il *he; it* (m)
île (f) *island;* **les îles Anglo-Normandes** *Channel Islands*
ils *they* (m); **ils sont** *they are*
il y a ... *there is/are ...*
immédiatement *immediately*
imperméable (m) *raincoat*
impossible *impossible*
imprimante (f) *printer*
incendie (m) *fire (blaze)*
indigestion (f) *indigestion*
infection (f) *infection*
infirmier, (fem) infirmière *nurse*
information (f) *information*
informations (f pl) *news (TV)*
ingénierie (f) *engineering*
ingénieur (m) *engineer*
inhabituel *unusual*
insecte (m) *insect*
insomnie (f) *insomnia*
instrument de musique (m) *musical instrument*
intelligent *clever*
intéressant *interesting*
internet (m) *internet*
interprète (m) *interpreter*
interpréter *to interpret*
interrupteur (m) *switch*
intoxication alimentaire (f) *food poisoning*
invitation (f) *invitation*
invité(e) *guest*
irlandais(e) *Irish*
Irlande (f) *Ireland*
Italie (f) *Italy*
italien(ne) *Italian*
ivre *drunk*

J

jamais *never*
jambe (f) *leg;* **jambe cassée** (f) *broken leg*
jambon (m) *ham*
janvier *January*

jardin (m) *garden;* **jardin public** (m) *park*
jardinerie (f) *garden centre*
jaune *yellow*
jazz (m) *jazz*
je *I;* **je suis** *I am;* **je voudrais** *I would like*
jeans (m pl) *jeans*
jeu (m) *game;* **jeux vidéos** (m pl) *computer games*
jeu de cartes (m) *pack of cards*
jeudi *Thursday*
jeune *young*
joli *nice; pretty (place etc)*
jouer *to play*
jouet (m) *toy*
jour (m) *day*
journal (m) *newspaper*
joyeux anniversaire! *happy birthday!*
juillet *July*
juin *June*
jupe (f) *skirt*
jupon (m) *slip*
jus (m) *juice:* **jus d'orange** *orange juice;* **jus de fruit** (m) *fruit juice*
jusqu'à *until*
juste *right; fair (correct);* **ce n'est pas juste** *it's not fair*
juste un peu *just a little*

K, L

kilo (m) *kilo*
kilomètre (m) *kilometre*
klaxon (m) *horn (car)*
la *the (fem)*
là *there;* **il n'est pas là** *he's out*
là-bas *over there*
lac (m) *lake*
lacet (m) *shoelace*
laid *ugly*
laine(f) *wool*
laisse (f) *lead*
lait (m) *milk*
lames de rasoir (f pl) *razor blades*
lampe (f) *lamp;* **lampe de bureau** *reading lamp;* **lampe de chevet** *bedside lamp;* **lampe de poche** (f) *torch*
landau (m) *pram*
langouste (f) *crayfish (saltwater)*
langue (f) *language; tongue*

lapin (m) *rabbit*
laque (f) *hairspray*
large *wide*
lavabo (m) *basin (sink)*
laverie automatique (f)
launderette
lave-vaisselle (m) *dishwasher*
laxatif (m) *laxative*
le *the* (m)
leçon (f) *lesson*
lecteur de cassettes (m)
cassette player
léger *light (not heavy)*
légumes (m pl) *vegetables*
lent *slow*
lentilles *lenses* (f pl); **lentilles
rigides** *hard lenses*;
lentilles semi-souples
gas-permeable lenses;
lentilles souples *soft
lenses*
**lequel, (fem) laquelle: lequel? which?; n'importe
lequel** *either of them*
les *the (plural)*
lessive(f) *washing powder*
lettre (f) *letter*
leur: leur chambre
their room; **leurs livres**
their books
levée (f) *postal collection*
lever: se lever *to get up*
levier de vitesse (m)
gearstick
librairie (f) *bookshop*
libre *free* (at liberty)
lime à ongles (f) *nailfile*
limitation de vitesse (f)
speed limit
limonade (f) *lemonade*
linge (m) *laundry*
(clothes)
lingettes (f pl) *baby wipes*
liqueur (f) *liqueur*
liquide: payer en liquide
to pay cash
lire *to read*
liste (f) *list*
lit (m) *bed*; **lit d'enfant** (m)
cot
litérature (f) *literature*
litre (m) *litre*
livraison (f) *delivery*
livre (m) *book*; *pound (money,
weight)*
loin *far*
long, (fem) longue *long*
longueur (f) *length*
lotion solaire (f) *suntan
lotion*
louer *to rent*

lourd *heavy*
luge (f) *sled*
lumière (f) *light*
lundi *Monday*
lune (f) *moon*; **lune de miel**
honeymoon
lunettes (f pl) *glasses*;
lunettes de soleil
sunglasses
Luxembourg (m)
Luxembourg

M

ma: ma maison *my
house*
machine à laver (f) *washing
machine*
maçon (m) *bricklayer*
Madame *Mrs*
Mademoiselle! *waitress!*
magasin (m) *shop*; **magasin
d'antiquités** *antique
shop*
magnètoscope (m) *VCR*
mai *May*
maigre *thin*
maillot de bain (m)
*swimsuit; swimming
trunks*
main (f) *hand*
maintenant *now*
mairie (f) *town hall*
mais *but*
maison (f) *house*
maître de conférences (m)
university lecturer
malade *ill*
mal à estomac (m) *stomach
ache*
mal à la tête (m) *headache*
mal de dents (m) *toothache*
mal de ventre (m) *stomach
ache*
manche (f) *sleeve*
Manche: la Manche
Channel
mandarine (f) *tangerine*
manger *to eat*
manteau (m) *coat*
maquillage (m) *make-up*
marché (m) *market*
marcher *to walk*
mardi *Tuesday*
marée (f) *tide*
margarine (f) *margarine*
mari (m) *husband*
mariage (m) *wedding*
marié *married*
marmelade d'oranges (f)
marmalade

marron *brown*
mars *March*
marteau (m) *hammer*
mascara (m) *mascara*
mât (m) *mast*
match (m) *match (sport)*
matelas (m) *mattress*;
matelas pneumatique
air mattress
matin (m) *morning*
mauvais *bad; poor (bad
quality)*; **mauvais herbes**
(f) *weeds*
mécanicien (m)
mechanic
médecin (m) *doctor*
médicaments (m pl)
medication
médicine (m) *medicine
(subject)*
**Méditerranée: la
Méditerranée** (f)
Mediterranean
méduse (f) *jellyfish*
meilleur: le meilleur
the best
melon (m) *melon*
même *same*; **le/la même ...
the same ...**; **la même
chose, s'il vous plaît** *the
same again, please*
menu (m) *set menu*
mer (f) *sea*
merci *thank you*
mercredi *Wednesday*
mère (f) *mother*
mes: mes chaussures
my shoes
message (m) *message*
messagerie (f): **messagerie
électronique** *email*;
messagerie téléphonique
voicemail
messe (f) *mass (church)*
métro (m) *underground*
mettre *to put*
meublé *furnished*
meubles (m pl) *furniture*
micro-ondes (m)
microwave
midday *noon*
miel (m) *honey*
mieux *better*
milieu (m) *middle*
mince *thin*
minuit *midnight*
minute (f) *minute*
miroir (m) *mirror*
mobylette (f) *moped*
mode (f) *fashion*
modem (m) *modem*

moi *me;* **c'est moi** *it's me;*
c'est pour moi;
it's for me; **c'est à moi**
it's mine
moins *less*
mois (m) *month*
mon: mon livre *my book*
moniteur (m) *monitor*
(computer)
monnaie (f) *change*
(money)
monsieur *sir;* **Monsieur** *Mr*
montagne (f) *mountain*
montant de tente (m)
tent pole
monter *to get on* (bus etc)
montre (f) *watch*
monument (m) *monument*
morceau (m) *piece*
mordre *to bite* (dog)
morsure (f) *bite* (by dog)
mort *dead*
mot (m) *word;* **mot**
de passe (m) *password*
moteur (m) *engine* (car)
moto (f) *motorcycle*
mou *soft*
mouche (f) *fly* (insect)
mouchoir (m) *handkerchief*
mouchoirs *tissues*
mouillé *wet*
moules (f pl) *mussels*
mourir *to die*
mousse (f) *mousse* (hair);
mousse à raser (f) *shaving*
foam
moustache (f) *moustache*
moustique (m) *mosquito*
moutarde (f) *mustard*
mur (m) *wall* (outside)
mûr *ripe*
mûre (f) *blackberry*
musée (m) *museum;* **musée**
d'art *art gallery*
musicien (m) *musician;*
musicien des rues *street*
musician
musique (f) *music;* **musique**
classique *classical music;*
musique folklorique *folk*
music; **musique pop** *pop*
music

N

nager *to swim*
natation (f) *swimming*
navette (pour aéroport) (f)
airport bus
né(e): je suis né(e) en ...
I was born in ...

nécessaire *necessary;*
ce n'est pas nécessaire
that's not necessary
négatif (m) *negative*
(photo)
négociant en vins (m) *wine*
merchant
neige (f) *snow*
neuf *nine*
neuf, (fem) **neuve** *new*
neveu (m) *nephew*
nez (m) *nose*
ni: ni un ni autre *neither of*
them; **ni ... ni ...** *neither ...*
nor ...
nièce (f) *niece*
nier *to deny*
noir *black*
noix (f) *nut* (fruit)
nom (m) *name;* **nom**
de famille (m) *surname*
nombre (m) *number*
(amount)
non *no*
nord (m) *north*
nos: nos enfants *our*
children
notre: notre maison
our house
nouer *to tie*
nourriture (f) *food*
nous *we;* **nous deux** *both of*
us; **nous sommes** *we are;*
c'est à nous *it's ours;* **c'est**
nous *it's us;* **c'est pour**
nous *it's for us*
nouveau, (fem) **nouvelle**
new; **de nouveau** *again*
nouvelles (f pl) *news*
novembre *November*
nudiste (m) *nudist*
nuit (f) *night*
nulle part *nowhere*
numéro (m) *number*
(figure)

O

objectif (m) *lens* (camera)
objets trouvés (m pl) *lost*
property
obturateur *shutter*
(camera)
occupé *busy* (occupied)
octobre *October*
odeur (f) *smell*
œil (m) *eye*
œuf (m) *egg*
oignon (m) *onion*
oiseau (m) *bird*
olive (f) *olive*

omelette (f) *omelette*
oncle (m) *uncle*
ondulé *wavy* (hair)
ongle (m) *nail* (finger)
onze *eleven*
opérateur (m) *operator*
(phone)
opération (f) *operation*
opticien (m) *optician's*
or (m) *gold*
orage (m) *thunderstorm*
orange (f) *orange* (fruit,
colour)
orchestre (m) *orchestra; stalls*
(theatre)
ordinateur (m) *computer;*
ordinateur portable (m)
laptop
ordonnance (f) *prescription*
ordre du jour (m) *agenda*
ordures (f pl) *litter; rubbish*
oreille (f) *ear*
oreiller (m) *pillow*
orgue (m) *organ* (music)
os (m) *bone*
ou *or*
où? *where?*
oublier *to forget*
ouest *west*
oui *yes*
ouvert (adj) *open*
ouvre-boîte (m) *can*
opener
ouvrir *to open*

P

page (f) *page*
paiement (m) *payment*
pain (m) *bread;* **pain grillé**
(m) *toast*
paire (f) *pair*
palais (m) *palace*
pâle *pale*
palmes (f pl) *flippers*
panier (m) *basket*
panne (f) *breakdown* (car); **je**
suis tombé en panne *I've*
had a breakdown
pansement (m) *plaster*
pantalon (m) *trousers*
pantoufles (f pl) *slippers*
papa *dad*
papier (m) *paper;* **papier à**
lettres *writing paper;*
papier cadeau *gift wrap;*
papier d'emballage
wrapping paper; **papier**
filtre *filter paper;* **papier**
hygiénique *toilet paper*
paquet (m) *package, packet*

par: **par avion** *air mail*; **par chemin de fer** *by rail*; **par exemple** *for example*; **par nuit** *per night*
parapluie (m) *umbrella*
parasol (m) *sunshade*
parce que *because*
parcours de golf (m) *golf course*
pardon!, pardon? *excuse me!; sorry! (apology); pardon?*
pare-brise (m) *windscreen*
pare-chocs (m) *bumper*
parents (m pl) *parents*
paresseux *lazy*
parfait *perfect*
parfum (m) *perfume*
parking (m) *car park*
parler *to speak, talk*; **parlez-vous ...?** *do you speak ...?; ...* **je ne parle pas ...** *I don't speak*
paroi (f) *wall (inside)*
parterre de fleurs (m) *flowerbed*
parti (m) *party (political)*
particulièrement *especially*
partout *everywhere*
pas *not*; **pas beaucoup** *not many*; **pas encore** *not yet*; **il n'est pas ...** *he's not ...*
passage (m) *driveway*
passager (m) *passenger*
passeport (m) *passport*; **passeport d'animaux** (m) *pet passport*
passe-temps (m) *hobby*
pastilles pour la gorge (f pl) *throat pastilles*
pâtes (f pl) *pasta*
patinoire (f) *ice rink*
patins à glace (m pl) *ice skates*
pâtisserie (f) *cake shop*
pauvre *poor (not rich)*
payer *to pay*
pays (m) *country (state)*; **pays de Galles** (m) *Wales*
pêche (f) *peach*; *fishing*: **aller à la pêche** *to go fishing*
peigne (m) *comb*
peigner *to comb*
peinture (f) *paint; painting*
pelle (f) *spade (shovel)*
pellicule couleur (f) *colour film*
pelouse (f) *lawn*

pendant *during*
pendule (f) *clock*
penser *to think*
pension complète (f) *full board*
père (m) *father*
perle (f) *pearl*
permanente (f) *perm*
permis (m) *licence*; **permis de conduire** (m) *driving licence*
personne *nobody*
petit *small*
petit ami (m) *boyfriend*
petit déjeuner (m) *breakfast*
petite amie (f) *girlfriend*
petite-fille (f) *granddaughter*
petit-fils (m) *grandson*
petits pois (m pl) *peas*
pétrole (m) *paraffin*
peut-être *maybe; perhaps*
phares (m pl) *headlights*
pharmacie (f) *chemist's*
photo (f) *photograph*
photographe (m/f) *photographer*
photographier *to photograph*
piano (m) *piano*
pickpocket (m) *pickpocket*
pièce (f) *coin; play (theatre)*
pièces de rechange (f pl) *spare parts*
pied (m) *foot*
piéton (m) *pedestrian*
pile (f) *battery (torch)*
pilote (m) *pilot*
pince (f): **pince à épiler** *tweezers*; **pince à linge** *peg*; **pince à ongles** *nail clippers*
pinceau (m) *paintbrush*
pipe (f) *pipe (for smoking)*
pique *spades (cards)*
pique-nique (m) *picnic*
piquer *to bite (snake), sting (insect)*
piquet de tente (m) *tent peg*
piqûre (f) *bite (snake); sting (insect); injection*
pire *worse, worst*
piscine (f) *swimming pool*
piste (f) *runway; ski slope*; **piste pour débutants** *beginners' slope*
pistolet (m) *pistol*

piston (m) *piston*
pizza (f) *pizza*
placard (m) *cabinet*
place (f) *room (space); seat; square (in town)*
plafond (m) *ceiling*
plage (f) *beach*
plaisanterie (f) *joke*
plan (m) *town map*
plancher (m) *floor (ground)*
plan de travail (m) *worktop*
plancher (m) *floor (ground)*
plante (f) *plant*
plaque d'immatriculation (f) *number plate*
plastique (m) *plastic*
plat *flat (level)*
plateau (m) *tray*
plats (m pl) *main courses*; **plats préparés** (m pl) *ready meals*
pleurer *to cry (weep)*
plombage (m) *filling (in tooth)*
plombier (m) *plumber*
plongeoir (m) *diving board*
plonger *to dive*
pluie (f) *rain*
plus *more*: **plus de** *more than*; **plus tard** *later*; **plus ou moins** *more or less*
plusieurs *several*
plutôt *quite*
pneu (m) *tyre*; **pneu crevé** (m) *flat tyre*
poche (f) *pocket*
poêle (f) *frying pan*
poignée (f) *handle (door)*
poignet (m) *wrist*
poire (f) *pear*
poireaux (m) *leek*
poison (m) *poison*
poisson (m) *fish*
poissonnerie (f) *fishmonger's*
poitrine (f) *chest*
poivre (m) *pepper (and salt)*
poivron (m) *pepper (red/green)*
police (f) *police*
policier (m) *police officer*
politique (f) *politics*
pommade (f) *ointment*
pomme (f) *apple*
pomme de terre (f) *potato*
pont (m) *bridge*

porc (m) *pork*
porcelaine (f) *china*
port (m) *harbour; port*
porte (f) *door* (building);
  porte d'embarquement
  (f) *gate* (at airport)
porte-bagages (m) *luggage
  rack*
portefeuille (m) *wallet*
porte-monnaie (m) *purse*
porteur (m) *porter*
portière (f) *car door*
porto (m) *port* (drink)
possible *possible*; **dès que
possible** *as soon as possible*
poste (f) *post; post office*
poster (m) *poster* (inside);
  (verb) *to post*
pot d'echappement (m)
  exhaust (car)
poubelle (f) *rubbish bin*
poudre (f) *powder*
poulet (m) *chicken*
poupée (f) *doll*
pour *for*; **pour moi** *for me*;
  pour une semaine *for a
  week*
pourboire (m) *tip* (money)
pourquoi? *why?*
pousser *to push*
poussette (f) *pushchair*
pouvoir *to be able*; **je peux
  avoir ...?** *can I have ...?*;
  vous pouvez ...? *can
  you ...?*
préférer *to prefer*
premier *first*; **premier
  étage** (m) *first floor*;
  première classe *first class*;
  premiers soins (m pl)
  first aid
prendre *to take*; **prendre le
  train** *take the train*;
  prendre un bain *have a
  bath*
prénom (m) *first name*
près de *near*; **près de
  la porte** *near the door*;
  près de la fenêtre *by the
  window*
préservatif (m) *condom*
presque *almost*
pressé: **je suis pressé** *I'm in
  a hurry*
pressing (m) *dry cleaner's*
prêt *ready*
prêtre (m) *priest*
prie: **je vous en prie** *you're
  welcome*
printemps (m) *spring*
(season)

prise (f) *plug* (electrical);
prise multiple *adaptor*
prise de sang (f) *blood test*
privé *private*
prix (m) *price*; **prix d'entrée**
  admission charge; **prix du
  billet** (m) *fare*
problème (m) *problem*
prochain *next*; **la semaine
  prochaine** *next week*
produit pour la
  vaisselle (m)
washing-up liquid
produits de beauté
  (m pl) *cosmetics*
produits entretien
  (m pl) *household products*
produits laitiers (m pl) *dairy
  products*
produits surgelés
  (m pl) *frozen foods*
professeur (m) *professor;
  teacher* (secondary)
profession (f) *profession*
profond *deep*
promener: **aller se
  promener** *to go for
a walk*
propre (adj) *clean*
prudent *careful*;
  soyez prudent! *be
careful!*
public (m) *public*
puce (f) *flea*
pull (m) *sweater*
punaise (f) *drawing pin*
pyjama (m) *pyjamas*

Q

quai (m) *dock; platform*
qualité (f) *quality*
quand? *when?*
quarante *forty*
quart (m) *quarter*
quatorze *fourteen*
quatre *four*
quatre-vingt *eighty*
quatre-vingt-dix *ninety*
quatrième *fourth*
que *than*
quel âge avez-vous?
  how old are you?
quelle heure est-il? *what's
  the time?*
quelque chose *something*
quelque part *somewhere*
quelquefois *sometimes*
quelqu'un *somebody*
quelqu'un d'autre *someone
  else*

qu'est-ce que c'est? *what's
  that?; what is it?*
question (f) *question*
queue (f) *queue*
qui? *who?*
quincaillerie (f) *hardware shop*
quinze *fifteen*; **quinze jours**
  fortnight

R

radiateur (m) *heater;
radiator*
radio (f) *x-ray; radio*
radis (m) *radish*
rafraîchissements
  (m pl) *refreshments*
raie (f) *parting* (in hair)
raisin (m) *grape*; **raisin sec**
  (m) *raisin*
rallonge (f) *extension lead*
ramer *to row*
rames (f pl) *oars*
randonée (f) *hiking*
rapide *fast; quick*
rapport de police (m) *police
  report*
rare *rare* (uncommon)
raser: **se raser** *to shave*
rat (m) *rat*
râteau (m) *rake*
rayon (m) *aisle* (supermarket)
réception (f) *reception*
receptionniste (m/f)
  receptionist
réclamation de bagages (f)
  baggage claim
recommandé: **en
  recommandé** *registered
  post*
record (m) *record* (sports etc)
reçu (m) *receipt*
réduction (f) *discount*
regarde: **cela ne vous
  regarde pas** *it's none of your
  business*
regarder *to watch*
règle (f) *ruler*
rein (m) *kidney*
religion (f) *religion*
remercier *to thank*
remonte-pente (m) *ski lift*
remorque (f) *trailer*
rendez-vous (m)
appointment
rendre *to return* (give back);
  rendre visite *visit* (person)
repas (m) *meal*
repasser *to iron*
réponder (m) *answering
  machine*

reposer: se reposer to rest (relax)
reseignments (m pl) directory (telephone)
réservation (f) reservation
réserver to book, reserve
résistant strong (material)
respirer to breathe
ressort (m) spring (mechanical)
restaurant (m) restaurant
reste (m) rest (remainder)
retard (m) delay
retirer to withdraw
rétroviseur (m) car mirror
réunion (f) meeting
réveil (m) alarm clock
revenir to return (come back)
revue (f) magazine
rez-de-chaussée (m) ground floor
rhum (m) rum
rhume (m) cold (illness); **rhume des foins** (m) hay fever
riche rich
rideau (m) curtain
rien nothing; **ça ne fait rien** it doesn't matter
rire to laugh
rivière (f) river
riz (m) rice
robe (f) dress
robinet (m) tap (water)
rocher (m) rock (stone)
rock (m) rock (music)
roman (m) novel
rond round (circular)
rondelle (f) washer
rond-point (m) roundabout
room service (m) room service
rose (f) rose; pink (adj)
rôti roasted
roue (f) wheel
rouge red; **rouge à lèvres** (m) lipstick
rougeur (f) rash
rouleaux (m pl) curlers
roux red (of hair)
rue (f) street
rugby (m) rugby
ruines (f pl) ruins
ruisseau (m) stream (small river)

S

sa: sa maison his/her house
sable (m) sand
sac (m) bag; **sac à dos**
backpack; **sac à main** handbag; **sac de couchage** sleeping bag; **sac poubelle** bin liner
saignant rare (steak)
salade (f) lettuce; salad
salle (f) room; **salle à manger** dining room; **salle d'attente** waiting room; **salle d'opérations** operating theatre; **salle de bains** bathroom; **salle de conférences** conference room; **salle de radiology** x-ray departement; **salle des urgences** emergency departement
salon (m) living room
salut hi
samedi (m) Saturday
sandales (f pl) sandals
sandwich (m) sandwich
sang (m) blood
sans without; **sans plomb** unleaded
santé! cheers!
s'arrêter to stop
sauce (f) sauce
saucisse (f) sausage
saumon (m) salmon
sauna (m) sauna
savoir to know (fact); **je ne sais pas** I don't know
savon (m) soap
science (f) science
seau (m) bucket
sec, (fem) sèche dry
sèche-cheveux (m) hairdryer
seconde (f) second (of time)
seconde: en seconde second class
secrétaire (m/f) secretary
secteur (m) field (academic)
sécurité: en sécurité safe (not in danger)
seize sixteen
sel (m) salt
semaine (f) week
séminaire (m) seminar
sentir to smell
séparé (adj) separate
séparer to separate
sept seven
septembre September
sérieux serious
seringue (f) syringe
séropositif(ve) HIV positive
serveur (m) waiter

serveuse (f) waitress
service de pédiatrie (m) children's ward
serviette (f) towel
serviettes hygiéniques (f pl) sanitary towels
ses: ses chaussures his/her shoes
seul alone; single (one)
seulement only
shampooing (m) shampoo
short (m) shorts
si if; whether
SIDA AIDS
siège pour bébé (m) car seat (for a baby)
siège social (m) head office
silencieux quiet (person)
s'il vous plaît please
simple simple
sirop (m) syrup
site web (m) web site
six six
ski (m) ski; **faire du ski** to go skiing
skier to ski
slip (m) underpants
snack (m) snack
sœur (f) sister
soie (f) silk
soif: j'ai soif I'm thirsty
soir (m) evening; **ce soir** tonight
soirée (f) party (get together)
soit ... soit ... either ... or ...
soixante sixty
soixante-dix seventy
soldes (f pl) sale (at reduced prices)
soleil (m) sun
solution de trempage (f) soaking solution (for contact lenses)
sommeil (m) sleep
somnifère (m) sleeping pill
son livre his/her book
sonnette (f) bell (door)
sortie (f) exit
sortie de secours (f) emergency exit
sortir to leave
soucoupe (f) saucer
soûl drunk
soupape (f) valve
soupe (f) soup
souper (m) supper
sourcil (m) eyebrow
sourd deaf
sourire (m) smile; smile (verb)

souris (f) *mouse*
sous ... *below ...; under ...*
sous-sol (m) *basement*
sous-vêtements (f pl) *underwear*
soutien-gorge (m) *bra*
souvenir (m) *souvenir; remember* (verb); **je m'en souviens** *I remember;* **je ne me souviens pas** *I don't remember*
souvent *often*
sport (m) *sport*
stade (m) *stadium*
stagiaire (m) *trainee*
station (f) *underground station*
station de ski (f) *ski resort*
station-service (f) *petrol station*
statue (f) *statue*
steak (m) *steak*
store (m) *blind* (window)
stupide *stupid*
stylo (m) *pen;* **stylo-bille** (m) *ballpoint pen;* **stylo-plume** (m) *fountain pen*
sucette (f) *lollipop*
sucre (m) *sugar*
sucré *sweet* (not sour)
sud (m) *south*
suisse(sse) *Swiss*
Suisse: la Suisse *Switzerland*
supermarché (m) *supermarket*
supplément (m) *supplement*
suppositoire (m) *suppository*
sur ... *on ...*
sûr *sure*
survêtement (m) *track suit*
sweat-shirt (m) *sweatshirt*
sympathique *nice* (person)
synagogue (f) *synagogue*
syndicat d'initiative (m) *tourist office*

T

ta: ta maison *your house* (singular informal)
tabac (m) *tobacco; tobacconist*
table (f) *table*
tablette de chocolat (f) *bar of chocolate*
taille (f) *size*
taille-crayon (m) *pencil sharpener*
talc (m) *talcum powder*
talon (m) *heel*
tampon (m) *tampon*

tante (f) *aunt*
tapis (m) *carpet;* **tapis de sol** (m) *groundsheet*
tapisserie (f) *tapestry*
tard *late;* **bus est en retard** *the bus is late*
tasse (f) *cup; mug*
taux de change (m) *exchange rate*
taxi (m) *taxi*
télé cablée (f) *cable TV*
téléphérique (m) *cable car*
téléphone (m) *telephone;* **téléphone portable** (m) *mobile phone*
téléphoner *to telephone* (verb)
télévision (f) *television*
témoin (m) *witness*
température (f) *temperature*
tempête (f) *storm;* **tempête de neige** (f) *blizzard*
temps (m) *weather; time;* **de temps en temps** *occasionally*
tennis (m) *tennis;* **les tennis** (m pl) *trainers*
tente (f) *tent*
terminal (m) *terminal*
terrain de camping (m) *campsite*
terrasse (f) *terrace*
terre (f) *land; soil*
tes: tes chaussures *your shoes* (singular informal; plural noun)
tête (f) *head*
thé (m) *tea*
théâtre (m) *theatre*
ticket (m) *ticket* (underground, bus)
timbre (m) *stamp*
tire-bouchon (m) *corkscrew*
tirer *to pull*
tiroir (m) *drawer*
tissu (m) *material*
toboggan (m) *toboggan*
toi: c'est à toi *it's yours*
toilettes (f pl) *toilets*
toit (m) *roof*
tomate (f) *tomato*
ton: ton livre *your book* (singular informal)
tondeuse à gazon (f) *lawn mower*
tongs (f pl) *flip-flops*
tonic (m) *tonic*
torchon (m) *dish cloth*
tôt *early*
toucher *to feel, touch*

toujours *always*
tour (f) *tower*
tourism (m) *sightseeing*
touriste (m/f) *tourist*
tourne-disque (m) *record player*
tournevis (m) *screwdriver*
tous les deux *both of them*
tousser *to cough*
tout *all; everything;* **tout droit** *straight on;* **tout le monde** *everyone;* **tout seul** *all alone*
toux (f) *cough*
tracteur (m) *tractor*
tradition (f) *tradition*
traducteur (m) *translator*
traduire *to translate*
train (m) *train*
tranquille *quiet* (street, etc.)
transpiration (f) *sweat*
transpirer *to sweat*
travail (m) *job; work*
travailler *to work*
traverser *to cross over*
trèfle *clubs* (cards)
treize *thirteen*
trente *thirty*
très *very*
tricoter *knit*
triste *sad*
trois *three*
troisième *third*
trop *too* (excessively)
trottoir (m) *pavement*
tu *you* (singular informal); **tu es** *you are*
tunnel (m) *tunnel;* **le tunnel sous La Manche** *Channel Tunnel*
tuyau (m) *pipe* (for water)

U

un/une *a; one;* **un/une autre** *another* (different)
université (f) *university*
urgence (f) *emergency*
urgent *urgent*
utensiles de cuisine (f pl) *cooking utensils*
utile *useful*
utiliser *to use*

V

vacances (m pl) *holiday*
vaccination (f) *vaccination*
vague (f) *wave;* faint (adj)
valise (f) *case*
valise (f) *suitcase*

vallée (f) *valley*
vanille (f) *vanilla*
vapeur: à la vapeur *steamed*
vase (m) *vase*
veau (m) *veal*
végétarien (adj) *vegetarian*
véhicule (m) *vehicle*
vélo (m) *bicycle;* **vélo tout terrain** (m) *mountain bike*
vendre *to sell*
vendredi *Friday*
venir *to come;* **je viens de ...** *I come from ...*
vent (m) *wind*
vente (f) *sale (transaction)*
ventilateur (m) *fan (ventilator)*
vernis à ongles (m) *nail polish*
verre (m) *glass*
verres de contact (f pl) *contact lenses*
verrou (m) *bolt (on door)*
verrouiller *to bolt*
vert *green*
veste (f) *jacket*
vêtements (m pl) *clothes*
vétérinaire (m) *vet*
viande (f) *meat*

vide *empty*
vidéo (f) *video (film/tape)*
vie (f) *life*
vieux, (fem) vieille *old*
villa (f) *villa*
village (m) *village*
ville (f) *city; town*
vin (m) *wine*
vinaigre (m) *vinegar*
vingt *twenty*
violet *purple*
violon (m) *violin*
vis (f) *screw*
visage (m) *face*
viseur (m) *viewfinder*
visite (f) *tour; visit*
visiter *to visit (place)*
visiteur (m) *visitor*
vitesse (f) *gear (car); speed*
vodka (f) *vodka*
voile (f) *sailing*
voilier (m) *sailing boat*
voir *to see;* **je vois** *I see;* **je ne vois rien** *I can't see anything*
voiture (f) *car; train carriage*
voix(f) *voice*
vol (m) *flight*
volaille (f) *poultry*

volant (m) *steering wheel*
voler *to fly; steal;* **on a vo.** *it's been stolen*
volet (m) *shutter (window)*
voleur (m) *thief*
vomir *to be sick (vomit)*
vos: vos chaussures *your shoes (singular formal; plural; plural noun)*
votre: votre maison *your house (singular formal; plural; singular noun)*
vouloir *to want;* **je veux** *I want;* **vous voulez?** *do you want?*
vous *you (singular formal; plural);* **vous êtes** *you are*
voyage (m) *journey*
vrai *true*
vue (f) *view*

W, Y, Z

wagon-lit (m) *sleeper*
wagon-restaurant (m) *restaurant car*
whisky (m) *whisky*
yaourt (m) *yoghurt*
yeux (m pl) *eyes*
zoo (m) *zoo*

...ledgments

... would like to thank the following for their help in the preparation of this book:
...e Miller for the organization of location photography in France; Hôtel-Restaurant,
...elais", Fontenay le Comte; Gare Routière de Fontenay le Comte; Pharmacie Parot, Nieul
...Autise; Garage Gouband, Oulmes; Musée de l'Abbaye de Nieul Sur L'Autise (Cabinet
...rac, Nantes); Boulangerie des familles, Coulon; Fromagerie, rue St Marthe, Niort; Fruits et
Primeurs Benoit, Halles de Niort; Gare SNCF de Niort; Magnet Showroom, Enfield, MyHotel,
London; Kathy Gammon; Juliette Meeus, and Harry.

Language content for Dorling Kindersley by G-and-W publishing
Managed by Jane Wightwick
Editing and additional input: Pamela Wightwick, Christine Arthur, Leila Gaafar
Additional design assistance: Phil Gamble, Lee Riches, Fehmi Cömert, Sally Geeve
Additional editorial assistance: Kajal Mistry, Paul Docherty, Lynn Bresler
Picture research: Louise Thomas

Picture credits

Key: t=top; b=bottom; l=left; r=right; c=centre; A=above; B=below

p2 Alamy: Ian Dagnall; p3 DK Images: Peter Wilson: p4/5 Alamy: f1 Online tl; images-of-france tr; Alamy RF: Andy Marshall bl; DK Images: br; Neil Lukas tcr; p6/7 Laura Knox: cl; p10/12 Alamy RF: BananaStock cAr; RubberBall cBl; Ingram Image Library: bl; p12/13 Alamy RF: John Foxx cAr; RubberBall br; DK Images: cl; Steve Shott cBr; Ingram Image Library: tr, cr; p14/15 Alamy: images-of-france tcr; Ingram Image Library: cAl, cl, cBl, cAr, cBr, bcr; p16/17 Alamy RF: RubberBall bcr; Ingram Image Library: tr; p18/19 DK Images: David Murray tr; Ian O'Leary clB; p22/23 DK Images: cl, Andy Crawford cAr; Susanna Price br; Magnus Rew tcrB; Ingram Image Library: bcl, tcr; p24/25 DK Images: clA, Dave King tcr; p26/27 Ingram Image Library: cl; p28/29 DK Images: Andy Crawford tcr; Dave King cr; Matthew Ward bclA; Ingram Image Library: bcrA, bcr; p30/31 Alamy RF: Comstock Images bcl; DK Images: cl, bclA; p36/37 DK Images: bcl, bcr; Magnus Rew cl; Ingram Image Library: bl; p38/39 Alamy RF: Imageshop / Zefa Visual Media cl; p40/41 Alamy: images-of-france bl; Alamy RF: Justin Kase cAr; DK Images: cl, bcr; p42/43 Alamy: Artografika Bildagentur cr; Alamy RF: Image Source tcr, cAr; Andy Marshall cAAr; p44/45 Courtesy of Renault: c; p46/47 Alamy: Artografika Bildagentur cr; images-of-france cl; Alamy RF: Imageshop / Zefa Visual Media br; DK Images: bcl; Ingram Image Library: trlB; Courtesy of Renault: tcr; p48/49 Alamy: Agence Images tcr; Ian Dagnall c; PCL bcr; Peter Titmuss cr; DK Images: bcl; p50/51 Alamy RF: Robert Harding Picture Library c; p52/53 Alamy: imagebroker cr; Alamy RF: Image Farm Inc cAr; Photov.com / Hisham Ibrahim tcrB; DK Images: cl; p54/55 Alamy: Frank Herholdt bcl; Jackson Smith cBl; Alamy RF: BananaStock cl; John Foxx c; Image Source cAr; ThinkStock tcr; DK Images: Andy Crawford bclA; p56/57 Alamy: Agence Images clA; Ian Dagnall cl; PCL tl; Peter Titmuss cAl; DK Images: clAA; Courtesy of Renault: bc; p58/59 Alamy: Michael Juno tcr; Alamy RF: Brand X Pictures cBl, cBBl; Image Source cAAl; DK Images: cAl; p60/61 Alamy: Robert Harding Picture Library bcr; Alamy RF: Image Source cAr; DK Images: Steve Gorton bl, tcrB; Pia Tryde cAAr; Ingram Image Library: cr; p62/63 DK Images: Stephen Whitehorn c; p64/65 Alamy: Arcaid bcrA; Alamy RF: GKPhotography cBr; Goodshoot cAAr; imagebroker c; Justin Kase tcrB; DK Images: Steve Tanner cAr; Ingram Image Library: tcr; p66/67 Alamy: Arcaid tl; Alamy RF: Image Source cAr; DK Images: tr; Stephen Whitehorn bl; Ingram Image Library: br; p68/69 Alamy RF: Balearic Pictures cr; f1 Online cBl; Doug Houghton cl; Indiapicture clB; Alamy RF: images-of-france cBr; Justin Kase bl; DK Images: Peter Wilson cAl; p72/73 Alamy RF: imagebroker tcrB; Image Source cAr; Comstock Images tcr; Avery Weight-Tronix: bl; p74/75 Alamy RF: Doug Norman bl; Ingram Image Library: c; p76/77 Alamy: Balearic Pictures cBl; f1 Online clB; Indiapicture bl; DK Images: Peter Wilson bcl; p80/81 Getty: Taxi / Rob Melnychuk bc; Ingram Image Library: cAr; Xerox UK Ltd: tcr; p82/83 Alamy: wildphotos.com tcr; Alamy RF: FogStock cAAl; Momentum Creative Group cAl; Shoosh / Up the Res cBl; Ingram Image Library: cl; p84/85 Alamy: Brand X Pictures cr; f1 Online c; Alamy RF: BananaStock bl; SuperStock tr; Ingram Image Library: crB; p86/87 Getty: Taxi / Rob Melnychuk tcr; p90/91 Alamy RF: Brand X Pictures tcr; DK Images: cl; David Jordan cAr; Stephen Oliver cr; Ingram Image Library: cBr; p82/93 Alamy RF: Pixland cr; DK Images: cl; Guy Ryecart tr; p94/95 Alamy: David Kamm cl; Phototake Inc bcl; Alamy RF: Comstock Images cr; ImageState Royalty Free bcr; DK Images: Stephen Oliver tcr; p96/97 Alamy RF: Pixland br; DK Images: tl; Ingram Image Library: tr; p98/99 Alamy RF: Bildagentur Franz Waldhaeusl bl; ThinkStock br; DK Images: Peter Kindersley cr; Getty RF: Photodisc Green c p100/101 DK Images: Steve Gorton tcr; p102/103 Alamy: The Garden Picture Library tcr; cAAr; Hortus b; D Hurst tcrB; Ingram Image Library: cAr; p104/105 DK Images: Paul Bricknell cl(6); Jane Burton bcl; Geoff Dann cl(2); Max Gibbs cl(4); Frank Greenaway cl(3); Dave King cl(1), cAr; Tracy Morgan cl(5); p106/107 Alamy: The Garden Picture Library br; DK Images: Peter Kinderlsey cr; p110/111 Alamy RF: RubberBall cr; DK Images: Andy Crawford cl; p112/113 Alamy RF: Image Source cl; DK Images: bl; Ingram Image Library: tcr; bcrA; p114/115 Alamy: FogStock tcr; David R Frazier Photolibrary, Inc cBr; Alamy RF: Image Source cAr; Index Stock cAl; DK Images: Max Alexander cr; p116/117 Alamy: The Garden Picture Library cAl; p118/119 DK Images: Steve Gorton tcr; GettyNews: Giuseppe Cacace c; p120/121 Alamy: ImageState / Pictor International cl; Alamy RF: Sarkis Images tcr; DK Images: cBl, bcl; Kevin Mallett br; p122/123 Alamy RF: BananaStock cA; Ingram Image Library: cl; p124/125 Alamy: ImageState / Pictor International bclA; DK Images: cBl, bcl; Paul Bricknell tc(5); Geoff Dann tc(3); Max Gibbs tc(1); Frank Greenaway tc(2); Dave King tc(4); Kevin Mallett bl; Tracy Morgan tc(6); p126/127 Alamy: imagebroker clB; Alamy RF: © Hisham Ibrahim / Photov.com blA; Image Farm Inc bl; p128 DK Images: Neil Mersh.

All other images Mike Good.